Take my yoke upon you, and learn of me; for I am meek and lowly in heart: and ye shall find rest unto your souls. Matt. XI 29.

THE SAVIOUR.

SACRED SCENES

AND

CHARACTERS.

BETHLEHEM.

J. T. HEADLEY.

NEW YORK.
JOHN S. TAYLOR

SACRED

SCENES AND CHARACTERS.

BY THE

REV. J. T. HEADLEY.

NEW YORK:
JOHN S. TAYLOR,
143 NASSAU STREET,
1851.

CONTENTS.

SACRED

SCENES AND CHARACTERS.

INTRODUCTION.

In my "Sacred Mountains," I endeavored to sketch some of those scenes which transpired on the hill-tops of Palestine. There are others, however, equally interesting, which have no such associations. Often as the reader contemplates these in imagination, the profoundest depths of the heart are stirred, and it seems *wrong* that we should never endeavor to portray them just as they must have appeared to the actors in them. We ought to remember that in the majority (I do not say all) of the cases in the Bible, where it is said the Lord did thus and so, no *direct* agency is intended—every thing transpired in accordance with natural laws, precisely as would now happen in similar circumstances. We are accustomed to speak of a pestilence, a shipwreck, or any great and sudden catastrophe, as the work of the Being who made us. The only difference between such events and those narrated in the Bible as the work of Heaven, is, that in the former the will and purpose of God *were revealed;* whereas to us they are hidden, and we are left to conjecture. They occur in the same *way*, but the causes why, and the end to be obtained, are not developed. Hence we make a great mistake when we read of those wonderful occurrences, and imagine them to be unlike those which constantly make up the world's history.

CHAPTER I.

THE RED SEA PASSAGE.

The last fearful night had come—the night of alarm, dread visitation, and death. The succession of terrible judgments sent on the haughty monarch of Egypt, had failed to subdue his imperious nature.

The rivers, streams, and rills of Egypt had been turned into blood, bearing on their crimson bosom masses of dead and dying fish. Insects and vermin had swarmed in every chamber and closet, dying where they had gathered, till an intolerable stench arose from the fetid heaps. Disease had seized on the cattle, sweeping them away by tens of thousands—a grievous plague smitten the people, and the voice of lamentation filled the air. A storm of thunder, hail, and fire, commingled, had burst on the land, the flames breaking in angry billows along the streets, and consuming every green thing in their devastating flow. A cloud of locusts, darkening the heavens in their endless flight, followed, devouring every tender blade that had shot forth since the passage of the storm, till a vast desert spread away where smiling fields had been. Darkness, such as could be felt, for three days covered the earth, and the decimated, diseased, and starving population trembled in affright, thinking that the last hour of time was about to strike.

Amid all this desolation and death, this

wreck of his empire, amid the prayers and maledictions of his suffering and distracted subjects, the iron-hearted monarch stood firm to his purpose. The captives that lay bound to his throne should not go forth free. Sternly defying God, he bore up under these accumulated woes with a resolution and will that astonish us. But now he was to be struck nearer home, the iron was to enter his own soul, and wring from thence the bitter cry of anguish and entreaty. The first-born in every house, from the first-born of the beggar to the heir-apparent to the throne, was to be smitten. Death in his grimmest form was to darken the door of every dwelling of Egypt; and the night of this dread visitation had now come. In the solemn hour of midnight, the angel of doom was to tread the quiet hamlet and the thronged city, and his icy hand be laid on one beating heart in every family, and its marble pressure force a death-shriek that should startle every sleeper there; and lo! twelve o'clock was striking. Three bright blood spots on the two door-posts, and the lintel of each door of the Israelites, showed that within dwelt a Hebrew, and said to the passing angel, "Enter not here." Humble tenements they all were, on which these crimson stains were placed; but they contained dwellers nobler and more sacred than the royal palace. It was midnight; and, as the last hour struck, a deep silence rested on the vast city. The tumult of the day and evening was over—the crowd had forsaken the streets, across which dim lights were swinging, and naught broke the solitude save the measured tread of the sentinel walking his nightly rounds, or the rumbling of a chariot, as some late reveler returned to his home. Here and there a light was seen in a solitary sick-chamber, giving to the gloom a sadder aspect, and out from a narrow alley would now and then burst the sounds of folly and dissipation. All else was still, for the mighty population slumbered as the sea sometimes sleeps in its strength. But suddenly; just as the "All's well" of the drowsy sentinel echoed along the empty streets, piercing shrieks rent the silence; and passing rapid as lightning from house to house, and blending in with each other, rung out on the night air with strange and thrilling distinctness. And then came a wail, following heavily after, and, rolling up around the palace, surged back over the trembling city. Unseen by mortal eye, the angel of death was treading with noiseless step the silent avenues and lanes, putting out one light in each household, and dismissing one spirit thence to its long home. In a moment the city was in an uproar; lights danced to and fro; the rapid tread of urgent messengers made the streets echo; the rattling of wheels was heard on every side; but still the wail of desolated houses rose over all, like the steady roar of the surge above the crash of the wreck.

In the midst of this scene of excitement and terror, the children of Israel took their flight. Nearly a million of them, their muffled tread shaking the earth, streamed through the darkness, and emerged into the open country. And when the morning dawned in the east, there lay the city before them, its towers and domes flashing back the beams of the rising sun in redoubled splendor. But what a change had passed over it since that sun last looked upon its magnificence. Sobs and cries arose from every door, for the dead lay in every dwelling.

In solid ranks the hundreds of thousands of Israel took up their line of march, and night found their tents spread on the edge of the wilderness. Far as the eye could reach, they dotted the open country around, and fringed, like a ridge of foam, the dark forest beyond. And when night fell on the scene, suddenly a solitary column of fire shot into the heavens, lighting up with strange brilliancy the forest and the encampment. There it stood, lofty as a tower that beetles over the sea, and inherent with light from base to summit. The white tents grew ruddy in the blaze, and the upturned countenances of the innumerable host, that gazed awe-struck on its splendor, shone as if they were standing under a burning palace. All night long, it blazed there in their midst and above them, illuming the desert, and shedding unearthly glory on hill, valley, and forest.

And, when the morning came, it turned into a column of snowy whiteness, revolving within itself like a cloud, yet distinct and firm as marble. No voice shook its thick foldings, yet it had a language more potent than that of Moses, and its silent command of "Forward," caused every tent to be struck, and set the vast host in motion.

Over the wide plain it moved in advance of the army, and through the deep gorges it rose far above the mountains—the strangest leader that a host ever followed. When the sun struck it, its long shadow fell across the massive columns in one unbroken beam, filling every heart with fear and dread. At night it stopped and stood still, like a single marble shaft, till darkness came down, and then it became again a shaft of fire.

Thus, day after day, they continued their march, plunging deeper and deeper in the wilderness, until at length word was brought that the enraged Pharaoh, with his entire army—chosen chariots and all—was in full pursuit. Consternation then filled every heart, and each eye turned anxiously to that mysterious pillar. But no change passed over its silent form; steady and calm as ever, it moved majestically forward, heedless of the thunder and tumult that were gathering in the rear. Perchance at night it did not stop as before, but moved on in the darkness, blazing along the desert, lighting it up with more than noontide splendor. On, on swept the weary host, while every moment nearer and louder roared the storm on its track. Still hoping, yet fearing and trembling, they followed that calmly-moving column, until, at last, it stopped on the shore of the sea. As they pressed up, despair seized every heart, for far away naught but a wide waste of water met their gaze, while the unchecked billows broke heavily along its bosom; and behind, rushing on, came the tens of thousands of their foes, panting for the slaughter. That fearful pillar of cloud and fire, then, was only sent to delude them to their ruin. Oh, what lamentations, and prayers, and murmurings, went up from the despairing host! They were on the desolate shore, against which the restless sea beat with a monotonous roar, while from the solitude arose the deafening roll of countless chariot wheels, rushing to the shock. All that night, the only obstacle between them and their enemies was that pillar of fire. Yet, slight as it seemed, it was more impregnable than a wall of adamant. Still it was a wild and fearful night; the morning must bring the onset and the slaughter; while, as if to heighten the terrors of the scene, a terrific wind arose, driving the sea into billows, that fell in thunder on the shore, and sounding as if God also was about to fight against them.

Thus passed this night of anguish and dread to the Israelites; but, when the morning dawned, lo! there opened the sea, like a mountain gorge—the green and precipitous sides standing in massive walls on either hand. "Forward," spake the cloud, and the stern command rolled in startling accents along the mighty column, and it descended slowly into the fearful depths. Like an army of insects they moved below, while the billows that broke along the surface of the deep, crested over the edge of the watery cliffs above them, as if looking down on the strange spectacle, and the spray that fell on their heads was the "baptism of the sea." The pursuers plunged into the same watery gorge, and as their rapid chariots drew near the fugitive host, it seemed for a while that the sea had been opened on purpose to entrap them, and make them fall easier victims to their foes. But at this critical moment, that strange cloud rose up, and moving back over the long line, planted itself in front of the Egyptian host. Its solemn aspect and mysterious form troubled the monarch and his followers, the wheels rolled from the axletrees of the chariots—the solid ranks became disordered and broken, and terror and tumult took the place of confidence and strength.

At length the fugitives, with their bleating flocks and lowing herds, ascended the opposite shore, and when the last one stepped upon the beach, that dripping cloud also moved up after them—and then, like a clap of thunder, the sea smote together and the wave rolled smoothly on as before. Swift-circling eddies and whirlpools, and huge bubbles of air bursting on the surface, alone told where the mighty host was buried, and where and how they struggled in the depths. At length the wreck began to heave upward, and oh! what an overthrow it revealed. Chariots and horses, and spears and shields, and myriads of corpses, darkened the sea as far as the eye could reach.

But what a spectacle that shore presented! the beach, the rocks, the hills, were all black with the living masses, as they stood, trembling and awe-struck, and looked back on the deep. For a long time not a sound broke the deathlike si lence that reigned throughout the vast throng. Each heart was full of dread and awe, as the heavy swells fell at their feet, casting on the beach, with heavy dash, broken chariots, whole ranks of men, now pale in death, and horses and weapons of war. There, too, stood the cloud, and looked on the scene, while on its white and lofty form, the eyes of the multitude ever and anon turned reverently from the piles of the dead below. But at last, joy and gratitude, and triumph at their great deliverance, gave way to the terror that had oppressed them; and suddenly there arose a shout louder than the thunder of the sea; "Sing unto the Lord, for he hath triumphed gloriously: the horse and his rider hath he thrown into the sea. The Lord is my strength and song, and he is become my salvation.—Who is like unto thee, O Lord, among the gods? who is like thee, glorious in holiness, fearful in praises, doing wonders?" From rank to rank—from ten times ten thousand lips, rolled on the mighty anthem, till the shore shook with the glorious melody, and the heavens were filled with the strain. And Miriam, with her prophetic face and eye of fire, separated herself from the multitude, followed by a throng of dark-haired maidens, on whose cheeks the glow of joy had usurped the pallor of fear; and as they moved in shining groups and graceful dances, their silvery voices rang out over the clash of timbrels and roar of the waves in triumphant bursts of music, and "Sing ye to the

Lord, for he hath triumphed gloriously: the horse and his rider hath he thrown into the sea," arose and fell like melody along the rivers of Paradise.

Fearful had been the pursuit, and great was the deliverance.

CHAPTER II.

ELI

ELI was a high priest of Israel, possessing great goodness of heart, but wanting firmness of purpose and energy of action. Of tender feelings and vacillating will, he appears to me like one who would rather submit his neck to the executioner's axe, than himself inflict the blow on one every way deserving his fate. This weakness of character was exhibited in the manner in which he educated his sons. He allowed their bad passions to grow unchecked, so that from wayward children they became wicked men. His conscience compelled him to reprove them, while he failed in energy to enforce his rebuke. This was the more culpable, since, as a high priest, his sons would necessarily themselves be priests, and hence it became him to see that they did not minister with impure hands. Instead of this, however, he let their evil tendencies have such scope, that, when they assumed the sacerdotal robes, they used their office for selfish ends, and the gratification of their base passions. When a man came to offer a sacrifice, they appropriated a great part of it to themselves, and insulted the women assembled at the door of the temple. So gross and open was their conduct, that the people turned with disgust from the sacrifice, feeling that no good could come from such mercenary and brutal priests. These enormities were told to Eli; but the doting old man only said, "Why do ye such things?—nay, my sons, it is no good report that I hear." A very safe remark of his, and no doubt fully appreciated by his contemptuous sons.

At length a man of God came to Eli, and placing before him his past conduct, and recounting in concise, but plain language, the solemn obligations that lay upon him, and the sin he had incurred in not restraining his vicious children, pronounced the doom of utter extermination on his family. Not long after, the same malediction was uttered by the Lord to Samuel, to which the old man bowed his head, saying, "It is the Lord; let him do what seemeth him good." He had done wrong, and he knew it, and now he would meekly suffer the penalty of his deeds.

Time wore on, and at length war was declared between the Israelites and Philistines, and a battle was fought, in which the former were beaten, with the loss of four thousand men. Attributing their defeat to the absence of the ark of the covenant, they sent for it, and Hophni and Phinehas, the sons of Eli, of course accompanied it. The two armies lay opposite each other, awaiting each the onset of his antagonist, when the Israelites saw the ark slowly approaching over the plain, the mercy-seat of solid gold glittering in the sunbeams. In a moment despondency gave way to courage, despair to triumph, and there went up a shout that rocked the mountains. "*The Ark of God! the Ark of God!*" rolled in deep Hebrew accents from tens of thousands of lips over the field of battle, sending terror and dismay to the hearts of the enemy. "What shout is that?" ran from lip to lip, and when it was told that the ark of the Lord was in the camp of Israel, they exclaimed, "We are lost! These are the mighty gods which smote the Egyptians, and strewed the way from Egypt hither with dead armies, and how shall we escape?" Their leaders, however, encouraged them, saying, "Be men, and fight bravely. Will you be the Hebrew's slave, as he has been yours? Quit yourselves like men!" Rousing their courage by such appeals they led them to the onset.

What a terrific sight did the battle-fields of old present! Not in solid columns, flanked by clouds of cavalry, and headed by fierce batteries, did they advance slowly to the work of death; but ten times ten thousand men rushed suddenly and savagely upon each other's bosoms, and the battle became so many fierce hand to hand contests. Hence it was longer protracted and more murderous than now.

As these two immense hosts, like two dark clouds, closed on each other, the shout of each drowned for a moment the braying of trumpets and clash of instruments of music. Straight on the ark of God went the Philistine thousands, bearing down every thing before them. Israel saw it, and all over the tumultuous field arose the cry, "*To the rescue!*" Begirt with ten thousand foes, the sacred emblem stood still on the plain, while that strong Hebrew shout rolled like thunder to the heavens, and the countless masses went pouring forward. Around the holy Shekinah swords dripping with blood flashed and waved, spears glanced, and banners rose and fell. The mercy-seat tottered to and fro in the doubtful fight—the cherubim shook, while clouds of dust rolled over the combatants, and all was rage, terror, and confusion. Wicked, but brave Hophni and Phinehas, true to their sacred trust, fell pierced with a hundred wounds, and the boldest of Israel's warriors sealed their fidelity with their blood. Vain valor—trampled under foot, borne backward by the on-rushing thousands, the defenders of the ark broke and fled. With a shout that fell like a death-knell on their brave spirits, their enemies seized the ark and bore it triumphantly away. Faint terror and utter despair seized every heart—the shriek rang out over the din of combat—"*The ark is lost! the ark is lost!*" and that magnificent host became a herd of fugitives, sweeping hither and thither over the plain. How well they fought, how freely they bled, we know from the fact that there fell of Israel that day *thirty thousand footmen.*

On this same terrible day of battle and of defeat, far off in the beautiful plains of Shiloh, sat an old man by the wayside, listening eagerly to every passing footstep. Bowed over his staff, with pallid cheek and lip, the venerable high priest of Israel was filled with gloomy forebodings. The ark of God, the idol of his heart, the more than his life, had gone to the dreadful battle-field. Ah! was the long-impending curse now to be fulfilled, and the approaching night to be the one which should close on him a withered trunk, with every green branch lopped away? Each passer-by regarded the blind old man with pity, and spoke cheering words, which fell on unheeding ears. His heart was far away with the host of Israel, and the ark of God, and on his dreaming, excited spirit, there came the noise of conflict and sounds of alarm. Thus he sat till evening; and as the glorious sun of Palestine stooped behind the western hills, flooding the valley below with beauty, his melancholy face took an expression of intenser anxiety. The gentle breeze lifted his thin silver locks from his temples, but still he sat like a statue cut from stone, and listened. Hour after hour had worn heavily away, but now, just as the last sunbeams fell in a shower of gold on his venerable head, the sound of hasty footsteps smote his ear. Not the startled deer lifts his head in more eager attitude than did that blind old man when first roused from his reverie by that rapid tread, which his heart foreboded too well, brought heavy tidings. It was one of the fugitives from the battle-field, still crimson with the slaughter—his clothes rent, and dust on his head, and despair in his eye. And lo! as he sped onward with the sad news, a cry of distress and anguish followed him. Eli heard it, and asked its meaning. The next moment the messenger of evil stood before him, and cried, "I am just from the army, and all is lost. Israel is fled before the Philistines, and her bravest lie dead on the field. Thy two sons, Hophni and Phinehas, are slain, and the ark of God is taken." Under the defeat of Israel, the patriarch bore firmly up: even the death of his two only sons did not shake his aged frame; but when it was told him that the ark of God was taken, he fell dead to the earth. All, all else could be borne: the slaughter of his people, his own and his sons' death, were nothing in comparison to the honor of his God. This last blow broke his heart as with a sudden crash, and he died without uttering his sorrow. Ah! who can tell the tide of feeling that swept over him at the fatal news? That his sins should be visited on the people and his sons, was natural—the prophetic curse had prepared him for this; but that the honor of God, which was dearer to him than life, should suffer for his misdeeds, was more than he could bear. The curse had struck deeper than he had anticipated, and in that day of terrible suspense, and in that moment of unspeakable anguish, he received the punishment of a fond but erring father.

Of a noble heart, full of all gentleness and love, pure and upright himself, yet he did not fulfil the responsibilities of a parent. His defects were rather mental than moral, and his crime consisted in not restraining others instead of not controlling himself. All his thoughts, wishes, and desires were pure, but he refused to arrest the vices of his children. Too easy in his temper, and doting in his affections, he would not see the evil he was bringing on them, on the people, and on himself. Thus does the fondness of parents, when allowed to blind their eyes to the faults of their offspring, or prevent them from punishing their misdeeds and checking their passions, always end in the misery of both. This is the lesson intended to be taught in this chapter of history, and it must be confessed that it is a fearful one, accompanied with fearful warnings.

How little we know of the designs of Heaven, and how completely contradictory do they often appear to passing events! Around that ark of God—the symbol of love and mercy—and for the silent tomb of the Son of God, who came to preach peace on earth, more blood has been shed than for any warlike banner that ever floated over a field of slaughter. The frightful wars of the Israelites, and the millions slain in the Crusades, to deliver the Holy Sepulchre, are strange facts in history. Yet the ordering of the one, and the permission of the other, are equally parts of that great plan whose origin is perfect wisdom, and whose result will be the greatest good that could be accomplished. The maudlin philanthropist of the present day, like Eli of old, cannot look upon severity or death, and would much rather crime should go unpunished, freedom fall, and justice be trampled under foot, than that men should be slain. These are they who would abrogate all law but that of kindness. To them, the Old Testament is an antiquated book, and the history of God's dealings with wicked men rather a curious relic of the barbarous past, than the stern and right action of their Maker and Judge.

CHAPTER III.

RUTH.

THERE seems no reason why the Book of Ruth should have been written, except to show the lineage of David. It is simply a sweet pastoral, a truthful tale, embodying the finest sentiments, and placing before us, in attractive colors, a young, lovely, and beautiful woman. It is a chapter in domestic life, told with charming simplicity, and awakening in the reader feelings of the purest and noblest kind. To one who reads the Bible in course, it comes like a sudden yet sweet surprise. The sterner feelings of his nature have been roused by the turbulent scenes of the Book of Judges. Fierce battles, private murders, and terrific slaughters, have followed each other in rapid succession. One of the last scenes that he dwelt upon, was the violent death of an unchaste woman, whose dismembered body was sent in bleeding fragments throughout the land, like the fiery cross of Scotland, to call men to arms, followed by the slaughter of a hundred thousand men, whose corpses strewed the fields—the whole closed by the forcible seizure of women for wives, like the rape of the Sabines.

From such a succession of horrors, the reader comes upon the simple and gentle story of Ruth, like one who emerges from an Alpine gorge, black with thunder-clouds, and filled with the roar of mad torrents, upon a little green pasturage, slumbering in the embrace of the hills, along whose quiet surface herds lazily recline or slowly wander, while the tinkling of bells mingling with the murmur of the streamlet, charms the soul into pleasure, seeming, from the very contrast, doubly sweet.

No novelist has ever been able, with his utmost efforts, to paint so lovely, so perfect a character as this simple story presents. From first to last, Ruth appears before us endowed with every virtue and charm that rendered a woman attractive. Naomi's husband was a man of wealth, and left Bethlehem to escape the famine that was wasting the land. In Moab, he found plenty, and there, with his wife and two sons, who married Ruth and Orpah, lived awhile and died. In the course of ten years, the two sons died also, and then Naomi, broken-hearted, desolate, and poor, resolved to return and die in her native land. How touching her last interview with her daughters-in-law, when she bade them farewell, and prayed that, as they had been kind to her and her dead sons, so might the Lord be kind to them. Surprised that they refused to leave her, she reasoned with them, saying that she was a widow and childless, and to go with her was to seek poverty and exile in a strange land. She could offer them no home, and perhaps the Jewish young men would scorn their foreign birth, and when she died none would be left to care for them or protect them. There they had parents, brothers, and friends, who loved them and would protect them. On the one hand were rank in society and comfort, on the other disgrace and poverty. Orpah felt the force of this language, and turned back; but Ruth, still clinging to her, Naomi declared that it was the act of folly and madness to follow the fortunes of one for whom no bright future was in store, no hope this side the grave. She sought only to see the place of her childhood once more, and then lie down where the palm-trees of her native land might cast their shadows over her place of rest. "Go back," said she, "with thy sister-in-law." She might as well have spoken to the rock;—that gentle being by her side, all shrinking timidity and modesty, whose tender feelings the slightest breath could agitate, was immovable in her affections. Her eye would sink abashed before the bold look of impertinence, but with her bosom pressed on one she loved, she could look on death in its grimmest forms unappalled. Fragile as the bending willow, she seemed, but in her true love, firm as the rooted oak. The hand of violence might crush, but never loosen her gentle clasp. With those white arms around her mother's neck, and her breast heaving convulsively, she sobbed forth, "*Entreat me not to leave thee,* for where thou goest I will go, and where thou lodgest, I will lodge; thy people shall be my people, and thy God my God: where thou diest I will die, and there will I be buried;—*naught but death shall part us.*"

Beautiful and brave heart! home, and friends, and wealth, nay, the gods she had been taught to worship, were all forgotten in the warmth of her affection. Tearful yet firm, "Entreat me not to leave thee," she said: "I care not for the future; I can bear the worst; and when thou art taken from me, I will linger around thy grave till I die, and then the stranger shall lay me by thy side!" What could Naomi do but fold the beautiful being to her bosom and be silent, except as tears gave utterance to her emotions. Such a heart outweighs the treasures of the world, and such absorbing love, truth, and virtue, make all the accomplishments of life appear worthless in comparison.

The two unprotected women took their journey on foot towards Bethlehem. It was in the latter part of summer, and as they wandered along the roads and through the fields of Palestine, Ruth, by a thousand winning ways, endeavored to cheer her mother. Naomi was leaving behind her the graves of those she loved, and, penniless and desolate, returning to the place which she had left with a husband and two manly sons, and loaded with wealth, and hence a cloud hung upon her spirit. Yet in spite of her grief, she was often compelled to smile through her tears, and struggled to be cheerful, so as not to sadden the heart of the unselfish, innocent being by her side. And at fervid noon, when they sat down beneath the shadowy palm to take their frugal meal, Ruth hastened to the neighboring rill for a cooling draught of water for her mother, and plucked the sweetest flowers to comfort her.

Thus, day after day, they traveled on, until at length, one evening, just as the glorious sun of Asia was stooping to the western horizon, the towers of Bethlehem arose in sight. Suddenly, a thousand tender associations, all that she had possessed and all that she had lost, the past and the present, rushed over her broken spirit, and she knelt and prayed, and wept. "Call me not," said she to the friends of her early days, who accosted her as she passed through the gates, "Call me not Naomi, or the pleasant, but Mara, *bitter*, for the Almighty hath dealt very bitterly with me."

Here again Ruth's character shone forth in its loveliness. She was not one of those all sentiment and no principle; in whom devotion is mere romance, and self-sacrifice expends itself in poetic expressions. Though accustomed to wealth, and all the attention and respect of a lady of rank, she stooped to the service of a menial in order to support her mother. With common hirelings she entered the fields as a gleaner, and without a murmur trained her delicate hands to the rough usage of a day-laborer. At night, her hard earnings were poured with a smile into the lap of her mother; and living wholly in her world of love, was unmindful of every thing else. Boaz saw her amid the gleaners, and struck with her modest bearing and beauty, inquired who she was. On being told, he accosted her kindly, saying that he had heard of her virtues, her devotion to her mother, and her self-sacrifices, and invited her that day to dine at the common table. With her long dark locks falling in ringlets over her neck and shoulders, and her cheek crimson with her recent exertions and the excitement at finding herself opposite the rich landlord, in whose fields she had been gleaning, and who helped her at table as his guest, sat the impersonation of beauty and loveliness. That Boaz was fascinated by her charms, as well as by her character, was evident. He had watched her deportment, and saw how she shunned the companionship of the young men who sought her acquaintance, and of whose attentions her fellow gleaners would have been proud. Nothing was too humble, if it ministered to her mother's comfort; but beyond that, she condescended to nothing that was inconsistent with her birth. Whether abashed by his looks and embarrassed by his attentions, or from her native delicacy of character, she arose from the table before the rest had finished, and retired. After she had left, Boaz told the young men to let her take from the sheaves without rebuke, and then, as if suddenly recollecting how different she was from the other gleaners, and that every sheaf was as safe where she trod as it would have been in his own granary, he bade them drop handfuls by the way, which she, wondering at their carelessness, gathered up. At sunset, she beat it out and carried it to her mother. Naomi, surprised at the quantity, questioned her closely as to where she had gleaned, and when Ruth told her the history of the day, the fond mother divined the whole. Her noble and lovely Ruth had touched the heart of one of her wealthy kinsmen, and she waited the issue.

The long conversations they held together, and the struggles of the beautiful Moabitess, before she could bring herself to obey her mother and lie down at the feet of Boaz, thus claiming his protection and love, are not recorded. Custom made it proper and right, but we venture to say that Ruth never passed a more uncomfortable night than that. Her modesty and delicacy must have kept her young heart in a state of agitation that almost mocked her self-control. The silent appeal, however, was felt by her rich relative, and he made her his wife. The devotion to her helpless mother—her self-humiliation in performing the office of a menial—the long summer of wasting toil—the many heart-aches caused by the rough shocks she was compelled, from her very position, to receive, at length met with their reward. Toiling through the sultry day, and beating out her hard earning at night, the only enjoyment she had known was the consciousness that by her exertions Naomi lived. It had been difficult, when weary and depressed, to give a cheerful tone to her voice, so as not to sadden her anxious mother-in-law; but still the latter saw that the task she had voluntarily assumed was too great, and therefore, at length, claimed from Boaz the obligations of a kinsman. Love, however, was stronger than those claims, and he took Ruth to his bosom with the strong affection of a generous and noble man. She thus arose at once to the rank for which she was fitted; and in time the beautiful gleaner of the fields of Bethlehem, became the great-grandmother of the King of Israel.

CHAPTER IV.

THE HAND-WRITING ON THE WALL.

One evening a royal form was seen walking on the terrace of his palace, and looking off upon the magnificent city at his feet. As his eye swept round the circuit of the walls, fifty miles in circumference, and three hundred and fifty feet high, and saw their hundred lofty gates of brass flashing in the sun-beams, and the hanging gardens suspended nearly four hundred feet in the heavens, loaded with shrubs and waving trees, and sparkling with fountains that leaped from beneath gayly decorated arches, and below on the wilderness of palaces and dwellings at his feet, his lips murmured, "Is not this great Babylon that I have built by the might of my power and for the honor of my majesty?" And well he might indulge in vain boasting, and believe that naught but an earthquake that should sink the land, could shake the city of his pride. Those massive walls, broad enough for eight or ten carriages to drive abreast upon them, rose higher than the loftiest spire of our land, till the clouds seemed to rest on their summit, while around a deep ditch was sunk filled by the Euphrates. Twenty-five gates of brass upon each of the four sides, with strong towers between, bade defiance to mangonel or battering-ram, while the boldest might shrink from scaling those slippery heights. Fifty streets, each a hundred and fifty feet broad and fifteen miles long, went from gate to gate, lined with palaces, and temples, and towers, and crowned with arches, till the eye ached with the magnificence and grandeur that met it at every turn.

But deep down amid these costly piles, was a far different scene. By the streams and fountains over which the willows wept, sat a band of Hebrew captives, their harps hanging silent upon the drooping branches, and their heads bowed in grief. To the gay promenaders who paused as they passed, and asked them to sing one of their native melodies, they replied with tears. In that strange land they could not sing, for their hearts were too full of Zion and her sad fate. They were the prisoners left from the spoils of Jerusalem; but their tears and prayers as they sat there, scorned and desolate, were shaking that proud city to its overthrow. Little did the haughty monarch think, as he looked on his stronghold, that the cries of those neglected captives were bringing down the lightning of heaven on its towers and battlements, and that to redress *their* wrongs fell at that moment the voice from heaven which startled him like a thunder-peal, "THY KINGDOM IS DEPARTED FROM THEE."

Years have passed by, and Nebuchadnezzar is in his tomb, resting in more than regal splendor, amid the despots who have gone before him; and another occupies his throne as haughty and wicked as he. Belshazzar too has heard, but not heeded, the first mutterings of the coming storm. The Persian thousands have swarmed for a long time around the city to overthrow it, and thundered on its massive walls and brazen gates in vain. Equally vain were the attempts to scale their heights from lofty towers of palm-trees; and so the baffled foe sat down to starve the impregnable city into subjection, and for two years had hedged it in with a wall of men. At this last attempt, also, the self-confident monarch laughs, for his granaries are stored with provisions for twenty years. The prophets may prophesy and the captives pray; he mocks at them all, and girdled in by his impregnable walls and fortresses, and surrounded by his myriad troops, he says: "*I will exalt my throne amid the stars of God.*"

It is a night of festivity, and the bacchanal's song and shout ring through the crowded streets of Babylon. Around her ancient towers, the reeling multitude cry hosannas to their gods. Wine flows like water, and lust and revelry walk the streets unchecked. In a magnificent palace, apart from the tumultuous crowd, the king is feasting a thousand of his lords. It is a gorgeous room, column within column, arch above arch, long corridors, magnificent statues, costly hangings, leaping fountains, and an endless profusion of ornaments combine to form a scene of such dazzling splendor, that the unaccustomed spectator is bewildered and lost in its midst. It is illuminated by lights from golden candlesticks, beneath which is spread a table loaded with golden vessels.

Princes and nobles, wives and mistresses, arrayed in splendid apparel—women whose beauty out-dazzles the splendor that surrounds them,—men of high renown—the gay, the voluptuous, and the proud are there, making the arches ring with their songs of revelry and shouts of mirth. Ever and anon come bursts of music, now swelling triumphantly out through the amplitude, and now dying away in soft and lulling cadences, while the perfume from burning censers is wafted in clouds over the intoxicated revellers.

At length the king, excited with wine, exclaimed, "Bring forth the vessels of gold that were taken from the Hebrews' temple;" and the servants brought them in. Gorgeous vessels they were, and as they stood upon the table covered with sacred emblems, and made holy by their dedication to the God of Heaven, they seemed to rebuke those who were about to profane them. But they only laughed, and filling them up with wine, drank confusion to the God of Israel, and "praised their gods of gold and silver and brass and stone." In the midst of their sacrilege, just as their mirth and madness had reached the highest point, there "*came forth fingers of a man's hand, and wrote upon the plaster of the wall.*" The sudden flash of that illuminated hand out-dazzled the brilliancy of the lighted room, and as the slowly-moving fingers silently traced the letters of fire before their eyes, terror and dismay fell on the revellers. The startled monarch turned paler than the marble beside him, the untasted goblet fell from his hand, and his knees smote together. Those loudest in their mirth suddenly grew silent as death; the seductive look became solemn and anxious,—the music stopped in the midst of its most joyous burst; and stillness, broken only by the half-suppressed shriek of the fainting, or the tremulous sigh of utter fear, reigned through the vast apartment. When the dread line was finished, the finger still pointed voicelessly to it, saying in language more impressive than the loudest thunder, "READ THY DOOM!" Oh! what a sudden change had passed over that hall of riotous mirth: every mouth was sealed, every eye fixed, and the upturned faces of the throng wore a ghastly hue in the light of that blazing hand and those letters of flame.

At length the king broke the silence, and cried aloud for his astrologers and wise men to read the mysterious writing for him. They gazed and turned away bewildered and terrified. Then Daniel, one of the Hebrew captives who had been brought a mere boy from Jerusalem, but had grown into favor with the monarch's father, interpreted his dreams and foretold his doom—was brought in. Turning to those fiery letters, written in his native language, he slowly read, "MENE MENE TEKEL UPHARSIN." Then looking steadfastly on the trembling, pallid king, he unfolded his crimes before him, and pointing above to the God he had scorned, whose mandates he had trampled under foot, he read aloud the doom written there in letters of fire on the walls of his own palace: "God hath numbered thy kingdom and finished it," for "thou art weighed in the balances and found wanting: thy kingdom is divided, and given to the Medes and Persians."

He turned away, and scarcely had the echo of his footsteps died along the silent corridors, when a distant murmur, like the far off sound of bursting billows arose over the city. It was not the tramp and shout of the drunken multitude. Sterner sounds than the hurrahs of revellers, and steadier footsteps than those of reeling men commingled there—the battle cry of charging thousands, and the measured tread of an army moving to battle. The Euphrates had been turned from its channel; and underneath the ponderous gates that closed over its waters, the Persian host had entered, and were now pouring in countless numbers through the streets. In a moment the vast city was in an uproar, and from limit to limit rung the cry of "*to arms, to arms!*" and trumpets pealed, and banners waved, and swords clashed, while shouts and shrieks swelled the tumult that gathering force at every step, now rolled like thunder up to the very gates of the palace. The streets ran blood; and borne back before the steadily advancing foe, the weary and mangled fragments of the royal army made a last stand, at the palace gates of their master. He too turned at bay, and throwing himself amid his guard, made one brave effort for his throne. Overborne and trampled under foot, he soon fell amid his followers, and the excited conquerors streamed through the royal apartments. They entered the hall of the revellers; and the sacrilegious fell where a moment before they had shouted for their gods. The wine goblets still stood on the table, and the perfume still filled the room, but the *hand-writing* had disappeared, for its denouncing woe had been fulfilled. The illuminated and gorgeous apartment—the throng of princely feasters—the hand and characters of fire—the battle and the slaughter had succeeded each other with frightful rapidity, and now the silence of death succeeded all.

Over the sickening scenes of that terrible night we draw the veil of oblivion. A vast and thronged city taken by storm and given up to rapine and lust, is one of the few spectacles that make us abhor our race. But Babylon had fallen, and her glory gone for ever. In a few years a magnificent ruin was all that remained of her former splendor. Wild beasts and reptiles swarmed through her ancient palaces—the owl hooted in the presence chamber of kings, and the vampire flapped his wings in the apartments once occupied by the beautiful and the proud. Her strong towers and battlements slowly crumbled back to their original dust, and silence and desolation reigned, where once the hum of a mighty population had sounded. The dust of the desert has long since covered the very ruins, and the Arab now carelessly spurs his steed over the foundations of the former glory of the world.

Turn back your eye for a moment a hundred years before this great overthrow. On the hills of Palestine stands a man whose prophetic eye pierces the future, and whose tongue of fire proclaims in language that thrills the blood, the coming doom of Babylon, the mistress of the world. (Isaiah xiii. and xlvii.) He sees his people carried away captive by her—Jerusalem laid in heaps—the Holy Temple plundered of her treasures, and the God of his fathers held in derision. As he contemplates all this, and then looks beyond and sees the day of vengeance, his soul takes fire, and he pours forth in the loftiest strains of poetry that sublime ode which has no equal on earth. A chorus of Jews first come forward and sing their astonishment at the overthrow of their oppressor. *How hath the oppressor ceased! the golden city ceased!* "When the whole earth breaks forth into singing," and the fir-trees and cedars of Lebanon join the anthem, shouting "*since thou art laid low, no feller is come up against us.*"

The scene then changes to the regions of the dead, and by the boldest figure ever introduced into poetry, the long line of the departed monarchs of Babylon are made each to start from his sepulchre, where they have reposed in ghastly rows for ages, and as they move towards the mouth of the gloomy cavern to welcome the last of their race, they chant to the fallen king. "Hell from beneath is moved to meet thee at thy coming—it stirreth up the dead for thee, all the chief ones of the earth; it hath raised up from their thrones all the kings of the nations." "Art thou," they exclaim in derision, "become weak as we? Art thou become like unto us? Thy pomp is brought down to the grave—the worm is spread under thee and the worms cover thee." This funereal and scornful welcome being over, the people of God again break in with the triumphant apostrophe, "How art thou fallen from Heaven, oh Lucifer, son of the morning! how art thou cut down to the ground that did'st weaken the nations!"

A hundred years before the downfal of this vast empire, while Babylon ruled the world, was this sublime and prophetic ode sung by Isaiah. The skeptic may deride the prophecy, but he cannot escape the effect of the sublime language in which it was uttered. The opening of Byron's great ode to Napoleon is a weak imitation, or rather poor paraphrase of it.

> "Tis done—but yesterday a king
>   And armed with kings to strive—
> And now thou art a nameless thing!
>   So abject—yet alive!
> Is this the man of thousand thrones,
> Who strewed our earth with hostile bones,
>   And can he thus survive?
> Since he miscalled the Morning Star,
>   Nor man, nor fiend hath fallen so far."

CHAPTER V.

SAMUEL AND SAUL.

THE INTERVIEW BETWEEN THE LIVING AND THE DEAD.

ONE evening, just as the sun was setting over the hills of Palestine, a host was seen encamped in a beautiful valley, through which wandered a clear stream, and over whose green surface, woods and fields, and flocks and herds, were scattered in endless variety and profusion. The white tents dotted the landscape far and wide, standing against the green background distinct as a fleet of snowy sails against a storm-cloud on the sea; while long rows of chariots glittered between, and gay standards floated above, and groups of officers and ranks of soldiers moved about, giving animation and life to the scene. At intervals came triumphant bursts of music; and the thrilling strains of the trumpet arose and fell over the plain, till the echoes were lost in the woods beyond. And the evening sun was shining on all this, tipping the tents of thousands of lance-points with silver, and flashing back from burnished armor till the eye became dazzled with the splendor.

On a gentle eminence that overlooked this glittering plain, was spread the tent of the king. Of ample dimensions, and decorated with gorgeous hangings and costly ornaments, it looked like a fairy palace there upon the swelling hill-top.

Underneath its spreading canopy sat the monarch himself, looking thoughtfully upon the prospect below him. It was a scene to stir a warrior's heart, for every one of those countless tents that stood bathed in the sunlight, contained soldiers true and tried; and all the vast host at his feet was but a single instrument in his hand. At the blast of his trumpet, that plain would tremble under the tread of armed men, twice ten thousand lances shake in the departing sunbeams, and, at his command, rank upon rank would rush all steadily upon a stand of leveled spears. They had often crowded after him to battle, had stood a wall of iron about him in the hour of peril; he had heard their shout of defiance ring over the clash of arms and tumults of the fray—ay, and their shout of victory, too, louder than all, as they drove the broken and shattered forces of the enemy before them. Well, then, might the sight of that tented host send the flush of pride to the monarch's brow, and fill his heart with exultant feelings.

But, alas, no color came to that marble face; pale and anxious the chieftain sat and gazed, his brow knit in gloomy thought, and care resting like a cloud upon his countenance. No food had passed his lips all day, yet something more than fasting had wrought that haggard look and bowed that regal head. The white tents sprinkling the field, the chariots beside them, the shining ranks of warriors, the triumphant strains of music, the glorious landscape smiling in the setting sun, the hum of the mighty host, were all unheeded. He saw them not, he heard them not; his troubled soul was busy amid other scenes, struggling with far other thoughts. The past and the future shut out the present. Another army arose before him—a host of sins, in ghostly array, in whose dread aspect no relenting could be seen. And, worse than all, the oracles of God were dumb; to his earnest questioning no response had been given; the Urim and Thummim ceased to be irradiated at his call, and silence and darkness rested on the ark of God. And now, as he thought of his crimes, and the silence of God, and of the battle on the morrow,

"Coming events cast their shadows before,"

and he saw his army routed and slain, and himself and his throne trampled under foot. No wonder the waving banners below him brought no glow to his wan and wasted features.

As the last light of day disappeared, and the fires began to be kindled in the broad encampment, he entered his tent, and, putting on a disguise, stole forth, and, as a last resort, turned his steps towards the house of a sorceress, and asked that Samuel might be raised from the dead.

THE INTERVIEW.

Scarcely had his request been made when a stately form arose before him clad in a dark mantle, his long gray locks and beard falling upon his breast and shoulders. It was Samuel — the same Samuel who had anointed him king over Israel, and for so long a time been the pillar of his throne; the dread and fearless prophet who so often had withstood him to his face, and hurled the malediction of Heaven upon him; whose last curse, backed with the startling declaration, "The Strength of Israel will not lie nor repent," still rang in his ears. The frightened monarch stood dumb and powerless before the dread spirit he had evoked from the land of shadows, when the deep sepulchral tones of the prophet broke the silence, "Why hast thou disquieted me, to bring me up?" "I am sore distressed," murmured the king, "for the Philistines make war upon me, and God is departed from me, and answereth me no more, neither by prophets, nor dreams: therefore I have called thee, that thou mayest tell me what I shall do." "Wherefore," answered the spirit, "dost thou ask me, seeing the Lord has departed from thee and is become thine enemy?" He would only repeat over again the curse of former days; and his words fell like a funeral knell on the ears of the monarch, "The Lord hath rent the kingdom out of thy hand, and given it to thy neighbor David." Not only has the throne gone, but the dynasty closes with thee, and thy family is disinherited for ever for thy sins. Nor is this all: the battle to-morrow shall go against thee, for "the Lord will deliver Israel with thee into the hands of the Philistines; and"—the prophet's voice here made the heart of the listener stand still in his bosom—"and, to-morrow shalt thou and thy sons be with me." The thunderbolt had fallen, and the utter silence that followed was broken only by the shock of the king's body as he fell lifeless and headlong upon the earth. No shriek, no groan, told when and how deep the blow struck; that heavy fall was more startling than language.

The fearful apparition sunk away, and Saul was left alone with the night.

The next morning found the king in his tent, nerved for the worst; and to those who saw him, as his servants buckled on his armor, he appeared the same as ever, save that a deeper pallor was on his cheek than thought can ever give—the pallor of despair. Nevertheless, the trumpets were ordered to sound, and soon the plain shook with the preparation of arms. Chieftains, each with his retainers behind him, marched forth, prancing steeds and chariots of war followed, banners and lances and hemlets fluttered and flashed in the morning sunlight, and all was hope and confidence in the army. As the troops defiled before the royal tent, shouts of "Long live the king" rent the air. Ah, with what a sudden death-chill those shouts fell upon his heart; that host was going forth to be slaughtered, and that bright sun in its course was to witness the loss of his army, his throne, his sons, and his life. Perhaps he cheered his desponding spirit with the vain hope that God might yet be appeased, or that Samuel had spoken falsely; at all events, he was determined to battle nobly for his crown. As his guard closed sternly around him, the determination written on his brow betokened a bloody day, and a fierce struggle, even with fate itself.

The hostile armies met, and rank after rank, troop after troop, rushed to the onset. The Hebrew sword drank blood; and the shout of Israel went up as thrilling and strong as ever it rose from Mount Zion itself. And never before did their monarch lead them so steadily and fiercely on; or give his royal person so freely to the foe. But courage, and heroism, and desperate daring were alike unavailing; the sentence was writ on high, and Israel was scattered before her foes. Vainly did their leaders rally them again and again to the charge. Vainly did the three princes, the sons of Saul, call on their followers to emulate their example, as they threw themselves on the foe. Vainly did the king himself lead on his troops, while the blood from his wounded side trickled over his armor. God was against them all; and, discomfited and scattered, they fled on every side. The three sons of the king fell one after another, bravely battling for their father's throne and Israel's honor, till at last Jonathan, the bravest and noblest of them all, fell lifeless on the hill-side. The wounded monarch, hard hit by the archers, at last turned and fled for his life; but, finding no way of escape, he stopped, and commanded his armor-bearer to stab him to the heart, "Lest," said the dying man, "these uncircumcised come and thrust me through, and abuse me." His armor-bearer refusing to commit the horrid deed, he placed the hilt of his own sword upon the ground, and fell upon it. His faithful armor-bearer followed his example, and he and the king and his three sons lay corpses together on the mountain of Gilboa.

The prophecy was fulfilled—the curse had fallen—and morning once more broke on the land of Israel.

CHAPTER VI.

THE NAMELESS PROPHET.

THE hills and groves of Palestine, ever so beautiful to the traveller over its burning plains, were in olden times often selected as the building spots for altars and temples. The shadowy recesses gave solemnity to the imposing ceremonies of the priest, while the cool breezes that wandered through them, bathed in refreshing coolness the silent worshipers that gathered there.

In one of these delicious groves, on a beautiful day, a royal form was seen standing before a magnificent altar, around which stood images and vessels of gold in costly profusion. Clad in splendid apparel, he remained a moment contemplating the smoke of the incense, as it curled slowly upward, while the dense throng around darkened every avenue that led away in the distance. That royal personage was the head of the rebel house that had usurped the throne of David, and drawn every tribe but Judah after his banner. To complete his scheme of wickedness, he had made gods of gold, and plunged the people into the vices of idolatry. He knew that if they reverenced the God of Israel, their hearts would soon yearn again towards the house of David.

With his honors fresh upon him, and feelings of pride and triumph swelling his heart, he gazed long and earnestly at the smoking altar, when suddenly a shadow darkened the ground before him. With a quick and angry glance, he looked up to see who had dared thus presumptuously to intrude on his devotions. A grave, stern man, wrapped in a mantle, stood beside him, with his eye fixed stedfastly upon the altar. Paying no heed to the haughty monarch by his side—not even deigning him a glance—showing no reverence to the gods before him, he calmly, sternly surveyed the gorgeous fabric with its unholy sacrifice. Before the king could recover from his astonishment at this strange and sudden apparition, a voice broke the silence. Apparently unconscious of the presence of the king and his menials, wholly absorbed with the altar before him, he addressed it as if it were a living thing, "O altar, altar! thus saith the Lord, a child from the house of David, Josiah by name, shall yet sacrifice upon thee, and his offerings shall be these high priests that now burn incense, and men's bones shall be burnt upon thee. The Lord hath said it, thou shalt be rent, and the ashes poured out." The *altar alone* received his malediction, but the denouncing curse was meant for the king who worshipped there. It was a bold and fearful act, for he stood alone amid a throng of menials, who needed but the slightest signal to hew him in pieces. The monarch's astonishment gave way to uncontrolable rage at being thus defied and cursed by an unknown and powerless man; and he sprang forward to seize him. In an instant the outstretched hand fell withered by his side, and the altar parted in the middle, and the ashes were poured upon the ground. As suddenly as astonishment had given way to rage, did fear usurp the place of both; and the king, who a moment before was bent on taking his enemy's life, now tremulously begged for mercy. He besought him to restore the withered arm that hung lifeless by his side. Prayers and tears effected what threats could never have done; and the heart that seemed made of iron—so cold, and relentless, and fearless did it beat amid his foes—was instantly filled with the tenderest sympathy, and he restored to the humbled monarch his arm. In the fulness of his delight and gratitude, the king invited him to his palace and to his table, offering to load him with gifts.

But the nameless prophet refused, saying that he would not for half his palace; for the Lord had charged him saying, "Eat no bread, nor drink water, nor turn again by the way thou camest." So he departed.

The singular appearance of this unknown man—his boldness—the fearful doom he had pronounced, and the miracles he had wrought, filled the beholders with amazement, and the news was spread on every side. Among others, the sons of an old prophet of the Lord brought the tidings to their father's ears. Instantly saddling his ass, he pursued after him—determined to know more of one who had uttered so fearful a malediction, and shown such high authority for it. He found him sitting by the way-side, under a spreading oak, doubtless musing on the mission he had just fulfilled, and the Being who had made him the messenger.

The old prophet began immediately to urge him to go back and eat with him. But the nameless prophet replied, as he did to the king, that it was the explicit direction of the Lord that he should not eat bread nor drink water in that place. Finding all his entreaties of no avail against the command of the Almighty, he changed his plan, and told him that he too was a prophet of the Lord, and added, "An angel spake unto me by the word of the Lord, saying, Bring him back with thee into thine house, that he may eat bread and drink water." "But he lied unto him." This staggered the stranger; and though he thought it singular that the Lord should send two such contradictory messages, still one of his prophets, a venerable and revered man, would not state an untruth. What questions he put, and what falsehoods the old prophet uttered to sustain the first, we are not told. The whole question hinged on the single fact, whether God had altered his commands. Still it doubtless was with many misgivings that he at length admitted that it was really so, and consented to return.

As he reined his unwilling beast back, methinks his heart felt a sudden chill, and a gloomy foreboding darkened his spirit. *Perhaps* it was false; and he was provoking the curse of that God whom he would rather perish than disobey.

The two prophets, however, were at

length on their way back, and a venerable pair they were as they rode side by side, and conversed of those high themes which related to God and the fate of Israel. As the old prophet spoke of the revelations that from time to time had been made to him—of his solemn interviews with the Almighty, the heart of the stranger must have felt relieved of its doubts; and the fearful misgivings, which would ever and anon shake his soul, departed. This *was* a man of God, and had been sent to him to hasten his return.

At length they reached the old prophet's home, and entered his humble dwelling. Their beasts were unsaddled, and the anxious and officious host ordered dinner to be spread, to which he sat down with his guest. In the midst of pleasant cheer, and still pleasanter conversation, the hours wore rapidly on. The old prophet exerted all his powers to give zest to the entertainment, and for once disobedience seemed about to be crowned with blessings.

But suddenly — at the very moment when they felt most secure — a strange light illumined the old prophet's face, and flashed in fearful splendor from his eye. The Spirit of the Almighty—the true inspiration—had entered him, and, rising up before his astonished guest, who sat watching with the intensest anxiety this sudden change, he cried aloud: "Thus saith the Lord, forasmuch as thou has disobeyed the mouth of the Lord, and hast not kept the commandment he gave thee, but camest back, and hast eaten bread and drunk water in the place where he did say to thee, eat *no* bread and drink *no* water, thy carcass shall not come unto the sepulchre of thy fathers." Had a thunderbolt suddenly fallen at the feet of the prophet, he could not have been more astounded. On his own confession, his host had lied to him, and now, at his own table, pronounced the curse upon that disobedience of which he himself had been the author.

With a fallen countenance and a heavy heart, the doomed man saddled his ass and rode away. With his head bowed on his bosom, and his long beard sweeping his garments, he passed slowly along, heedless of all the objects around him. Weary and heavy was the way; for he knew the light of his dwelling would never more cheer his eye, nor the voices of those he loved fill his heart with delight. By the road-side his rejected body should be thrown, to be devoured, perchance, by the dogs; and, worse than all, the stigma of a wicked prophet would be fixed on his name for ever. Oh! who can tell the flood of anguish that then swept through his bosom, or the broken prayer to the God of his fathers which then arose from his crushed and broken spirit.

While he was thus passing sadly along, a lion sprang upon him, and slew him. But, held by an invisible hand from touching his prey, he, together with his ass, stood and watched over the corpse. Travelers turned in wonder from the strange spectacle, and brought the news to the city. The old prophet knew at once that it was the victim he had seduced to his ruin; and, filled with remorse and pity, he hastened to him, and taking up the corpse, brought it over to his own house. Mourning over it with tears, that came too late, he cried, "Alas, my brother!" And well he might, for that pale face in its death-stillness, uttered a reproach more touching than language, and all the ghastly wounds, "with their dumb mouths," pleaded like angels against the murderer. "Take him," said the stricken prophet, "and lay him in my grave, and when I am dead, then bury me in the same sepulchre; lay my bones beside his bones. Let the same sepulchre inclose us, and let the monument that tells of the disgrace of the one perpetuate the falsehood and crime of the other." It was all that he could do by way of atonement, and one tomb held the victim and the seducer. No name crowned the resting-place of the stranger; he was known only as the "Man of God," and for ages his sepulchre was the sepulchre of "THE NAMELESS PROPHET."

A fearful lesson this, to those who would forsake the command of God for the declarations of man.

CHAPTER VII.

JACOB.

THE whole history of Jacob is complicated as the plot of a play. Scheme involves scheme — one adventure succeeds another, and hair-breadth escapes, cunning management, and unexpected success, keep the reader in a state of constant excitement. The issue is all that could be wished; yet the means often used to bring it about are, to say the least, questionable, and quite irreconcilable with the principles of truth and virtue. Jacob and Esau were two brothers—the latter of whom, being the elder born, was entitled to all the privileges of birthright. Full of fire and daring, he loved the excitement of the chase, and was never more at home than when scaling the steep mountain side, in hot pursuit of game. His bold spirit, keen eye, and resolute will, pleased his father, who often ate of the venison he brought home from his hunting expeditions. Jacob, on the other hand, was a "plain man, dwelling in tents;" that is, he loved to be amid his flocks, and passed his days in the quiet occupation of a grazier. It was natural the father should love the former, and the mother the latter. Jacob's gentleness and home feelings pleased Rebecca more than the rough and stormy nature of Esau.

On one of his hunting expeditions, Esau had been tempted to a longer and sharper pursuit than usual, and when he at length on his return drew near his brother's tent, he was weary and faint from his over-exertion and want of food. Seeing Jacob cooking a savory dish, he asked for some to eat. The latter, instead of generously offering him what he needed, took advantage of his distressed condition, and proposed that he should sell his birthright for a mess of pottage. Exhausted and starving, Esau consented, and the wily Jacob supplied his necessities.

Jacob's character presents strange and striking contrasts. Gentle and affectionate, he nevertheless in his youth seems to have been selfish and calculating. A generous impulse would have prompted him to succor his fainting brother without thoughts of reward. To bargain with a starving man, indicates a shrewd and calculating mind, but not an honorable spirit. On the other hand, Esau's willingness to part with blessings, temporal and spiritual, for the sake of the mere present and immediate gratification of his hunger, proves him to have been a man unworthy of his birth-right.

This, however, was only the first act in the drama. When Isaac had become blind in his old age, and felt that he must soon die, he called Esau, and bade him go and kill him a deer, and cook it, and afterwards he would give him his last blessing. Rebecca overheard him, and immediately, with her son, concocted a plan so full of fraud and falsehood, that we turn away, almost appalled to find it successful. Jacob was aided to kill a kid, which she disguised so skilfully, that the old man believed it to be venison, and then covering her son with the skin, to resemble the hairy form of Esau, bade him go in and cheat his father. This he did; and when Isaac, staggered by the voice, which had none of the abrupt and rough tones of his elder brother, asked him directly if he were Esau, he not only declared that he was, but piously attributed to God his success in having obtained the venison so soon. With this direct falsehood burning on his conscience, he coldly heard the blessing of his blind and misguided father. One would think the blessing would have turned into a curse, or at least in the eye of Heaven, which judges not by outward appearances, that the *intention* would have been taken for the *deed*, and, as the blessing was *designed* for Esau, so he should have received the benefits of it. Not so, however. This seems strange to us, at first sight, and we wonder how a just God could sanction such fraud by allowing it to be successful. But we must remember that Esau had lost all claim to the birthright, for he had sold it for "a mess of pottage." He had parted with his right so recklessly, that it was evident that the priceless treasures bound up in it were unsafe in his hands. At any time, he might barter them for a morsel of food or a quaff of wine. Not only this, but his character was every way unfit for the responsibilities and obligations his birthright conferred upon him. On the other hand, the very means, so desperate and extraordinary, which Jacob took to receive the blessing, showed that he would prize it above all other good. In the estimation of its value, therefore, he stood before his elder brother. In general character he certainly was far superior.

But, granting both to be equally unworthy of it, one by the contempt in which he held it, and the other by his fraud and falsehood: who had the *best claim?* The fixed law of succession *must* prevail, for all the hopes of a Saviour rested upon it; and granting the acts of both to have been wrong, on the side of which of the two did the balance fall? By the strict code of justice, evidently on that of Jacob. But when we put into the scale the general character of Jacob, all doubt is removed. Our difficulties arise from the fact, that Jacob seems unworthy of what he received, forgetting that man's salvation depended on him or Esau receiving this very blessing.

As one must have it, Jacob was the man; and his *absolute* unworthiness is not to be taken into the account; for if unworthiness forfeited the blessings of Heaven, where should we all be? It is the *selling* them for a mess of pottage—throwing of them away at the impulse of passion, that causes the shipwreck of our hopes. To err in our *anxiety*—to sin in our *eagerness* to obtain them, may be pardoned; but *contempt* of them, never.

The whole matter may be thus re-stated. The birthright was precisely what an entailed estate now is, which must fall on one or the other of the sons, or be thrown away, and the benevolent plans of God thwarted. Since, therefore, one must reap the advantages of it, to which of the two should they be given? On the ground of strict legality, to Jacob, most certainly, for he had purchased it—it was his by contract. On the score of *merit*, he had at least an equal claim — on that of character, the best. Who, then, would decide differently, if in his power? Who would give it to Esau, and oh, who would throw it away? The whole difficulty lies in the fact that fraud was successful. We forget that in such a case the success by no means proves the deception to have been sanctioned. Jacob *had won*, but for the means used he was afterwards to pay dearly. At the time, however, he did not probably look on the crime as so great. He had purchased the birthright just as he would have done a tract of land, and therefore considered it his. Yet he knew the strong hand of Esau would certainly rob him of it, and he must keep his own by management, or lose it. His fraud was practised to retain what was legally his own, not to wrong another. Thus he doubtless considered it, and although it does not show a particularly nice conscience, it glosses over the transaction.

From the agitating scenes around his father's sick-bed, and from the dark and wrathful brow of Esau, who sought his life, Jacob fled to his uncle Laban, living in Haran. A lonely wanderer, he lay down at night under the open sky and slept, and lo! the heavens opened above him, and radiant steps unfolded till they reached the earth, down which angelic beings came in shining groups, while a voice of mercy cheered him with glorious promises.

At Haran, however, he was paid off somewhat for the deception he had prac tised on his father. Falling in love with his beautiful cousin, Rachel, he engaged to work seven years for her. Unwearied and faithful, he entered resolutely upon the fulfilment of his contract; and as the long probation wore slowly away, his heart swelled with joyful anticipations. The beautiful being before him, on whom every thought and feeling was centered, for whom he had toiled so long and anxiously, was soon to be his for ever. At length the last day of toil came, and as the sun sunk behind the western hills, and night stole over the earth—the night which was to place Rachel in his embrace—joy and rapture awoke in his heart. The seven years seemed now but a day, and worthless compared to the treasure within his reach. Alas! next morning, instead of clasping

Rachel in his arms, he found that Leah had been imposed upon him by his uncle. The seven years were thrown away, and in that moment of heart-sickness and bitter disappointment and disgust, he felt that *deception* was a two-edged sword, that cuts both ways.

But here we meet again the brighter aspect of his character. Gentle in his nature, and relying more upon management than force—rarely giving way to impulse, but swayed by judgment, he nevertheless had a warm and affectionate heart. It was this, no doubt, which so endeared him to his mother. His love for Rachel was lasting as life—indeed, life was worthless to him without her, and he cheerfully toiled seven years more to obtain her. A spirit so sacrificing, and a love so deep and abiding, reveal a nobleness of character seldom seen.

His management, however, again exhibited itself, in obtaining his just wages from Laban, and his timidity when, in his flight from his father-in-law, he met his brother Esau. Fearing the vengeance of the latter, he endeavored, by flattery and presents, to turn him from his purpose, and succeeded. So, also, his religious character is seen in the faith and earnestness with which he wrestled in prayer till he prevailed, and thus obtained the name of Israel.

All along, there start forth those little incidents which reveal, like a sudden flash, the whole horizon of thought and feeling. Thus, when he met Esau, and was still uncertain what his reception would be, the division of his little band tells where his heart was. Leah, and her maids and children, were put in advance, and Rachel and Joseph in the extreme rear, where the shock should reach last. And as, in those stormy, rough days, the strong hand of violence frequently seized first on woman as its prey, should it be so here, Leah and her maids might furnish victims enough, and his beautiful Rachel be spared.

Of his return, at length, to Canaan—of his interviews with Heaven, and the events that followed, we shall say nothing. Rachel, in giving birth to another son, Benjamin, died; and Jacob was left to mourn her loss.

The more interesting passages of his life we shall speak of in connection with Joseph.

CHAPTER VIII.

THE DREAM AND ITS FULFILMENT; OR, JACOB AND JOSEPH.

THERE is nothing in the whole range of human history or romance so full of strange occurrences and touching incident, as combine to bring about the fulfilment of Joseph's dreams. He was the son of Rachel, whom Jacob always designated by the appellation "*My wife*"—the *other* was none of his choosing, and hence had none of his love. As it was natural, after the death of his wife, his affection all concentrated in her two children. Joseph was the eldest, and beautiful as he was brave and good.

The old man could not conceal his partiality for the boy, and lavished on him the choicest presents in his power to bestow, and decked him out in a gay coat—thus selecting him from all his brethren to receive the special marks of his favor. Their hatred and envy on this account were greatly augmented when he, in his innocence, related two dreams; one in which their sheaves stood up around his sheaf, and made obeisance to it; and the other, where the sun, moon, and stars did him reverence;—the only interpretation of which was, that he should be lord over his brethren, and honored even by his father.

So, once, whilst pasturing their flocks in Shechem, seeing Joseph—who had been sent by their father to inquire after their welfare—approaching, they said: "Here comes this dreamer: let us finish him at once, and see what will become of his dreams." Reuben interfered, on the ground that it was monstrous to shed the boy's blood, and persuaded them to fling him into a pit, doubtless with a view to liberate him privately. When the unsuspecting Joseph was first made to comprehend the full extent of the wrong meditated against him, he could hardly believe it true. But as they harshly stripped off his parti-colored coat, and roughly dragged him towards the mouth of the pit, he could no longer doubt, and begged most piteously for life. He besought them by the ties of brotherhood, for their father's sake, for *pity's* sake, not to cast him alone down that fearful abyss. His prayers and tears were alike unavailing, and they thrust him harshly into the dark entrance, and his agonizing shrieks gave way to low moans of despair.

At length, however, seeing a company of Ishmaelites passing by, they concluded to sell him; and then, dipping his coat in the blood of a kid, they took it back to their father, saying, "We found this in the field, all bloody and torn, as you see it;—is it Joseph's?" "Yes," replied the afflicted father, "it is Joseph's: a wild beast has devoured him." And he rent his clothes, and put on sackcloth, and mourned bitterly. All his friends endeavored to comfort him, but he repelled their sympathy, declaring he would go broken-hearted to his grave.

In the mean time, Joseph was taken to Egypt, and sold to one of the officers in the king's army. It is not common for the Bible to stoop to compliment one's personal appearance, but it says that "Joseph was a goodly person, and well-favored." Possessed of a fine, noble form, and handsome face, his manly beauty awoke the passions of his master's wife, and she persecuted him with base proposals. Finding all her approaches repelled, her love turned into hatred; and, with a lie too infamous to be placed in the catalogue of ordinary crimes, she charged him with assaulting her person. Hurled from his place of trust, and cast into prison without leave to defend himself, he suffered not only the miseries of a dungeon for two years, but the mortification of knowing that his character was ruined—his truth and virtue all gone in the eyes of the world. Ah! his brothers were right enough in calling him "a vain dreamer." His little role is played out, and the great world of strife and toil moves on without his prison walls, and he is forgotten for ever. Thus might he reason: but the sleepless eye of One above human events did not forget him. Pharaoh must have a troubled dream, and Joseph be the only one to interpret it. From the hard floor of a dungeon he mounts to the chariot of Pharaoh, and the neglected prisoner of a captain of the guard becomes first lord of all Egypt. Ah! when she saw him in the king's chariot, invested with regal power, how that false woman must have trembled for herself and husband. The man she had basely maligned and imprisoned, was now where he could strike *any* enemy down. His hour of revenge had come; and in the suspense she endured day after day, expecting her exposure and humiliation, she received the punishment of her crime. But Joseph cast her from his memory, as he would a reptile from his path, and bent all his energies during the seven years of plenty to hoard enough for the seven years of famine that were to follow. Why, in the plenitude of his power and success, he never sent to his father, to tell him of his existence and prosperity, we are not informed. Nor does it matter;—we only know that the complicated plot was not to end thus. That he thought of his father and his home—that he wished to know if he were still alive, and feared that he might die before he could weep on his neck, may well be imagined.

But time passed on, and by long famine the land was withered up—the crops failed, and the hoarded grain of the years that had passed was exhausted.

It is then, when the sons of Jacob came to Egypt to buy corn, that we for the first time begin to see how the tangled web of events is to be unraveled, and catch a glimpse of the way the riddle is finally to resolve itself.

Those envious brothers stand in presence of the lord of Egypt without recognizing him. *He* has changed since they tore him from their side, and dragged him shrieking to the pit. The beautiful boy has become the well-developed and noble man; and clothed, not in "a coat of many colors," but in the royal apparel of the chief man in the realm, he looks himself "every inch a king." But the shepherds of Shechem have not so changed—they look just as they did when he plead beseechingly for life, and he recognizes them at a glance. He has not forgotten the unspeakable anguish of the last moment his eyes fell upon them. As he turned to them, one after another, in his touching prayer for mercy, the face of each became daguerreotyped on his heart for ever. *He knows them*, and speaks harshly to them—they are spies—they are any thing but honest men. When, to repel this charge, they honestly told their history, and spoke of their family—referring to Joseph as dead, and Benjamin as with their father—he declared, by the life of Pharaoh, that he would not believe them, unless they brought that younger brother down. He imprisoned them three days, and then released them, on condition that one should remain bound with him, as surety that the rest should return with Benjamin. He spoke to them in Egyptian, and they, supposing he did not understand Hebrew, conversed with each other in an under-tone. Remorse had at length awoke, and self-reproach, and they said: "This is the punishment for having treated our brother Joseph so. We saw his anguish when he plead with us, but would not hear; and now his blood is required of us!" This was striking a tender chord in Joseph's breast, and calling back a whole world of associations. In a moment, Egypt, and Pharaoh's court, and his own glory, all disappeared from sight, and he saw only his father's white tent and the sweet fields of Canaan. Nature tugged heavily at his heart-strings, and the choking sensation in his throat told him that his self-control was fast vanishing before the swelling tide of fraternal and filial love, and he retreated hastily to his room. There, giving vent to his emotions in sobs and tears, he washed himself and returned.

When they again arrived at home, and told their father what had happened, the old man's fears were aroused, and he exclaimed, "Ye have bereaved me of my children: Joseph is dead, and Simeon gone, and now ye will take away Benjamin also. All these things are against me. He shall not go; for if any mischief befall him, you will bring my gray hairs with sorrow to the grave." Not to save Simeon will he risk Benjamin. They ceased entreating, and waited to see how the famine would affect him.

The little ruse the old man practised, some time after—so natural, and yet so easily detected—lets us into his character at once. After days and weeks had passed away, and want began to stare him in the face, he spoke in the most ordinary, indifferent manner, as if the whole affair of Benjamin had been forgotten—indeed, was not worth being referred to again, saying, "Go down into Egypt and buy more corn." "No," said Judah, "we cannot, we *will* not go without Benjamin." With the petulence and unreasonableness of old age, when it finds its structure of straw, reared with so much pains and cunning, suddenly demolished, he exclaimed, "Why did you tell him that you had a brother? Why deal so ill with me?"

It was useless, however, to contend with

famine. Without corn, Benjamin and all must die; and the troubled patriarch, after receiving the solemn oaths of his sons to bring him back, at last consented. To bless him and send him away, was a task almost too great for his strength. Joseph was long since dead, Rachel was dead, and Simeon a captive. The boy Benjamin—the child of his old age—the only relic of the wife he had so long and so deeply loved—the last nestling on the roof-tree to cheer the evening of his days—the only object that made the world bright to him, must then go to a foreign land, to meet, perchance, the fate of Simeon and of Joseph. How the doting father, when he found he could no longer shrink from the fatal blow, grasped at every thing that could add to the security of his child.

"Take," said he, "the choicest fruits of the land, and carry them down to the man as a present; and a little balm, and a little honey, and spices, and myrrh, and nuts, and almonds. Perhaps when he sees these little presents from the old man, he will pity his loneliness and be kind to his boy."

At length, after having done all within his power, he shook off, by a strong effort, the anxious parent, and rising to the dignity of the man of God, said: "Go, and God Almighty give you mercy before the man. If I be bereaved of my children, I am bereaved."

The light of his heart, the joy of his life, is at length gone. The patriarch stands in the door of his tent—his white locks falling on his shoulders—and watches the fair form of his boy receding in the distance, until at last a clump of trees shuts him from sight. Even then he does not turn away, but lingers a long time, gazing with an ashen cheek and tremulous lip on the spot where he last saw his idol; and then he bows himself in prayer to the God of his fathers. Oh! how he laid before him the promises he had made—how he pressed the pledge that had been given.

Wearily and sadly passed the days to Jacob; the nestling was gone from his bosom — the light of his tent departed. That tent was now desolate; the whole world looked lonely; his very herds moved sorrowfully over the fields; the sky, the clouds, the earth, had suddenly changed their aspect.

While Jacob and his sons are in this state of ignorance and suspense, it is pleasant to turn to Joseph, who alone manages the whole plot. But he had overestimated his self-control; for, when his brethren again stood before him, and gave him the presents and money of his father, and he saw Benjamin with them, his heart beat with a violence that mocked the mandates of his will. That beautiful boy, with his open, affectionate countenance, was "*his mother's son*," his only brother, and his whole nature reached forth towards him. He could only say, "Is this the brother of whom you spake?" God be gracious to thee, my son!" and rushed out of the room to hide the tears that could not be stayed. In the solitude of his chamber, he relieved his burdened heart, and returned with a composed mien into their midst. He had the whole of them with him at dinner;

yet even here his love, which clamored so loudly for expression, could not help revealing itself. He piled on Benjamin's plate—boy though he was—five times as much as on any of the others. The look of innocent wonder with which he met this extravagance, again and again brought the tears into Joseph's eyes. Ah! how blind they were, not to see that he was *devouring* that child with his looks, and that every motion was an effort to restrain himself from snatching him to his bosom.

Having passed this trial safely, he sent them away, with their sacks full of corn—ordering the steward to put the silver cup into Benjamin's sack, and then, as soon as they had left the city, to pursue after and charge them with stealing it. He did so; and the brothers, knowing themselves innocent, bade him search, saying that he in whose sack it was found, should be his lord's bondman for ever. Beginning at the eldest, he opened one sack after another with the same success, until at last none but Benjamin's remained. All anxiety had now ceased on their part, for they knew that little Benjamin could not steal. It was a mere matter of form, opening *his* sack; but lo! the first object that met their astonished eyes, was that glittering cup. Alas, alas! they had just been congratulating themselves on their good fortune. With plenty of corn, and Benjamin with them, they were on their return route to their father. Their fears had all given way to delightful contemplations, when lo! their hopes were thus suddenly dashed, and Benjamin, on their own conditions, was to be a bondman for life. With rent clothes and despairing hearts they returned to the city, and prostrating themselves before their lord, made no excuse, but offered themselves at once as slaves. This was all he could ask, and the worst was over. Not so. Joseph declared he would have none but the culprit—the rest might return to their father. What, go back without Benjamin! Such an alternative was worse than death, and Judah roused himself to one desperate effort to avert the catastrophe. Rising and approaching Joseph, he begged him not to be angry, but hear him; he then commenced a most tender, touching appeal to his feelings and his affections. Ah, *that was quite unnecessary;* poor Benjamin, as he stood silent and wretched, the innocent cause of all this misery, the tears trickling down his cheeks, was making that appeal with ten thousand tongues, till Joseph himself turned paler than his brethren. But, swallowing down by a convulsive effort his rising emotions, he stood with compressed lips, and knitted brow and heaving chest, awaiting the issue. Judah then went on to remind him that he had questioned them of their father and family; and when they had honestly told him all—even of their brother Benjamin, he had commanded them to bring him down to Egypt. Said Judah, "I told my father this, but he would not let him come. And when he besought us again to go and buy food we refused, unless Benjamin accompanied us. He replied, You know my wife bare me two sons, and one went out from me, and was torn in pieces, for I have never seen him since; and now if you take this one away also, and mischief befall him, you will bring down my gray hairs with sorrow to the grave." In this simple and earnest manner, he went on pleading for his aged father and for Benjamin, in such touching language, that the heart of a stranger would have melted. Joseph listened to the recital—saw the picture Judah drew of his father, and when he came to speak of how dearly that father still loved his long lost son Joseph, and the sorrow and wretchedness that now threatened his declining years, he could no longer restrain himself. The swelling tide of feeling that had so long been kept back, now rushed the wilder for the force that had been laid upon it, and he cried with a loud voice,

"Let every man leave me;" and he stood alone with his brothers. He then burst into a passionate fit of weeping, and sobbed so loud and convulsively, that the court of Pharaoh heard him. After the first gust of feeling had passed by, he exclaimed, "I am Joseph; doth my father yet live?" Had a thunderbolt suddenly fallen at their feet, they could not have been more astounded, and they stood silently looking on each other—while consternation, shame, remorse, and hope, agitated them by turns. But there was no place in Joseph's bosom for anger, and he endeavored to console them by saying it was all for the best that they had sold him. God had ordered it aright. He then snatched Benjamin to his bosom, and covered him with caresses, and the two brothers lay a long time in each other's embrace, weeping.

All this time, Jacob was counting the days that should bring Benjamin back; and when at last the little caravan heaved in sight, how his heart beat as he saw him riding safely in the midst. In the fulness of his joy at his safe return, Judah told him that Joseph was yet alive, and was lord of Egypt. The shock liked to have proved too much for his aged frame—the blood sallied back to his heart, and he fainted. When he at length revived, he said, "It is enough; Joseph my son is yet alive, I will go down and see him before I die." And he did go down, and Joseph came in his chariot to meet him. Of that interview we cannot speak. An aged father taking to his bosom a long-buried son, and a noble son murmuring on that bosom, in the midst of his tears, "*My father, my father,*" answered only by the tremulous "*God bless thee, my son,*" is one of the holiest sights this earth presents. The rapture of that moment compensates for years of pain. The Bible says that Joseph "*wept on his neck a good while.*" How simple the declaration, and yet how full of meaning. "*A good while!*" yes, the garnered affection of years, the hoarded treasures of the heart, all it had suffered and all it had hoped were not to be uttered in a short embrace.

THUS *was the double dream fulfilled.*

CHAPTER IX.

THE STAR OF BETHLEHEM.

LATE one night, when all was still around a rude hostelry in Judea, save, perchance, the rippling of the wind through the tree-tops, a young mother gave birth to a son. She was one of a company of poor travelers, who had taken up their night lodgings in the stable. Such a birth was no uncommon thing among the poorer classes; and yet Heaven never bent over a universe just rolled into being with such intense, absorbing interest, as it did over that unconscious babe, as it lay with feeble fluttering breath upon its mother's bosom. The heavens were quiet above—the inmates of the low inn slumbered peacefully—the shepherds were dreaming, free from care, amid their flocks on the fresh hill-sides, and all nature was at rest when the birth-throes of that fair young mother brought troops of angels from the throne of God.

But suddenly a change seemed to pass over nature—mysterious influences were in the air—the slumberers on the hill-side and in the valley felt a strange unrest, and arose and came forth into the open air. Whisperings were about them, and sounds like the passage of swift wings, all sweeping onward to one place, and then on the darkness of night a new star arose, bathing the landscape in mellow splendor, and flooding that rude inn and ruder stable with light that dazzled the beholder. There it stood, beautiful and bright, pointing with its steady beam to that slumbering babe. Encompassed in the still glory, the wondering shepherds turned in alarm one to another, but saw in the shining countenance of each only cause of greater fear. While they thus stood hesitating what to do, an angel hovered above them, saying, "Fear not, for behold I bring you good tidings of great joy, which shall be to all people: for unto you is born this day, in the city of David, a Saviour, which is Christ the Lord." Suddenly, crowds on crowds of radiant beings swept around them, singing, "Glory to God in the highest, and on earth peace, good will to men." Oh, how that glorious anthem arose and fell along the Judean mountains. "Glory to God in the highest!" from voices tuned in Heaven for ages to melody, and sent up in one exultant shout from that excited host, burst again and again on the ear. The heavens trembled with the song, and far away, beyond the reach of watching shepherds, or listening men, were louder shouts, and more entrancing melody.

With that shout and that song on their lips, the host of glad angels wheeled away to Heaven, and all was still again. But still that star kept shining on, and lo! the shepherds from the hill-tops, and wise men from afar, guided by its finger of light, came to where its beam fell on the infant in the manger, and worshipped him there. Strange occupants were in that stable. The wise and proud were there kneeling. Angels had been there adoring. The Son of God was there sleeping in a human mother's arms. That stable was greater than the palace of a king, for its manger cradled the "KING of kings, Emmanuel, The Wonderful, Counsellor, Prince of Peace, Redeemer, Saviour of men," were all embraced in that helpless infant. There it lay, calm, and fair, and lovely, the companion of cattle, and yet the Maker of the earth, and the adored of Heaven—the son of a carpenter, and the "Son of God." The feeble arm could scarcely lift itself to its mother's neck, yet on it the universe stood balanced. Its voice was faint, low, and infantile, and yet, at its slightest cry, myriads on myriads of angelic beings would crowd to its relief. A few hours measured its existence, and yet it lived before the stars of God. Born to die, and yet the conqueror of death. No wonder that star beamed on its face, for it did more than declare its heavenly birth, or direct the wise men to where it was cradled. It was pointing to the great solution of the problem of life, and of the profoundest mystery of Heaven. For four thousand years the world had summoned its thought and energies, and exhausted its wisdom on the single question, "How shall man be just with God?" The smoke of the first altar-fire kindled on the yet unpeopled earth, as it curled slowly heavenward, was burdened with this question. From the borders of deserted Eden—from the top of Mount Ararat—from the Bethel of Abraham, and from the tents of Jacob, had the sacrificial flame burned skyward in vain. The priests of Aaron had stood before the altar, and struggled for ages with the mighty problem, and lo! the "Star of Bethlehem" pointed to that babe as its solution. The long wanderings of the Hebrews — the miracles that preserved them — the imposing ceremonies of their religion—the "ark of God," the "mercy-seat," the pomp of temple worship, what did they all mean? That silent star pointed to the reply. Altars and sacrifices, prayers and prophecies, all were to end here. For four thousand years the earth had been rolling on its axis to bring about one event, and lo! it was accomplished. To the thousand inquiries of the human heart—to its painful questionings—to all its hopes and fears for so long a period, this was the answer and the end. Like a shadow for ever fleeing, had the mystery of justification baffled both the thoughtful

13

and inspired. The Hebrew with his temple worship and his offerings—the pagan with his heathen rites and his gods—the philosopher with his reason and his conscience, and the poet with his imagination, had pondered for ages over it. Watchings and fastings, self-humiliation, long pilgrimages, self-immolation, and death, had been cheerfully, nay, joyfully endured, to solve it. Too high for the rapt prophet, too deep for the sage, it still remained to sadden and excite the heart of man, till the "Star of Bethlehem" arose on the plains of Judea. Then the problem was solved and the mystery explained, but by One greater than all.

The long line of David, unbroken through so many centuries, was maintained solely to secure the birth of that child. Rapt in holy enthusiasm, Isaiah and Jeremiah, and all the prophets of God, had spoken of a King of Israel yet to come, whose throne should excel all the thrones of earth, and in the sublimest strains of eloquence spoken of the glory of his kingdom and the splendor of his reign. Through ages of oppression—through long years of captivity—from the depths of suffering, had prophets and people looked forward to the coming of the "Redeemer of Israel," and now, as if to mock their hopes, that silent star pointed to the babe of a carpenter's wife as the fulfilment of all.

Oh what a bitter disappointment, to be told that the King of Glory—the Prince of Peace—the Redeemer of Israel—the hope of the human heart, were in that infant, coarsely clad and laid in a manger.

Yet that star said more than all this.

To the longings after *immortality*—to the dim hopes—the painful bitter cry of the human soul after a *life to come*, it still cast its dazzling rays on that rude manger. The sad soul may question on and struggle on; but the sleeper there alone can satisfy its desires. It may range the fields of thought—exhaust all learning and all philosophy — dive into its own unfathomed depths; yet there alone is unfolded the mystery. "*Life and immortality*" are in that manger—so speaks the ever-beaming star. Kneel there with thy soul, which has fallen back exhausted from the fearful heights it has endeavored to climb unaided; fling thy philosophy, thy pride, as well as thy fears away, and let the light of that wondrous star fall on thy countenance, and its ray subdue and gladden thy spirit.

Painful doubts and appalling fears, lest the sinful heart could never be accounted pure —unsatisfied longings and shadowy visions of a life to come, are all over. Oh, with what thrilling eloquence that silent star spoke to the bewildered, melancholy race of men!

Not only did it point to the only way of justification, and reveal the life of the soul, when its earthy clog is cast away, but it shed light on the *grave of the body*—cast the first ray that ever fell within its dark and voiceless chambers. It said, as it shone, "Behold the resurrection and the life:" "There is the first-fruits of them that sleep." Wondrous beam, penetrating to the caverned head, casting unearthly splendor on the charnel-house, and flooding with light and glory the mutilated fragments which the worm and corruption have left. To the "whole creation, travailing in pain and groaning," waiting for the redemption of the body, it said, in accents sweeter than ever yet fell on mortal ears, "Be still—that babe shall open the portals of death, and lead captivity captive."

To the heavens above, it also spoke a language. It solved the mystery of redemption—showed how Mercy and Justice could be united; and revealed the length, and breadth, and depth, and height of the love of God—a length that reaches from everlasting to everlasting, "a breadth that encompasses every intelligence and every interest; a depth that reaches the lowest state of human degradation and misery, and a height that throws floods of glory on the throne and crown of Jehovah."

Two great events mark the long history of the earth. One is the coming of Christ in a human form as the "Babe of Bethlehem," to save and redeem—the other is to be his coming in the plenitude of his divinity to judge the world. A single star arose and beamed on his birth: at his second appearance, the stars of heaven shall all be quenched, the sun be "turned into darkness, and the moon into blood.

CHAPTER X.

THE DISCIPLE THAT JESUS LOVED.

THE lives of most men are on the same plan, marked by the same vicissitudes, checkered by the same light and shade, joys and sorrows. The same storms overhang their path; and, passing through similar sufferings, they drop, one like an other, over the same brink, into the echoless abyss of the grave. But now and then one appears, born to a different destiny. Thrown upon turbulent or rapidly changing times, he is impelled, by a violence he cannot resist, along dizzy heights and down frightful gulfs, until the long martyrdom is brought to a close by a death which changes the fate of an empire. Another, from childhood, goes only from mystery to mystery; revelations from on high, spirit voices singing in his ears, and unearthly visions dazzling his eyes, keep his soul in a state of fearful excitement, now thrilling with joy and now shuddering with fear. One-half of *his* sky is always too bright for mortal eye to gaze upon, and the other half, black with thunder clouds piled on thunder clouds. Thus it was with the prophets and priests of old, and with the inspired apostles of Jesus Christ. They dreamed dreams, they saw visions, they heard "the lyres of angels and the whispers of friends"—*they talked with God face to face.*

Most of these men, chosen for such a

high destiny, possessed characters of great energy and activity. John alone seemed made to love. Less fitted than Paul for the sterner struggles which accorded with the latter's nature, he wished ever to be reposing on the bosom, or receiving the caress, of his Friend and Master. Sentiment and sympathy predominated in him; he was a poet by nature; kind, generous, and full of emotion; and was happy only when surrounded by those he loved. Serene trust and immovable faith were his great virtues.

There is something inexpressibly touching in his attachment to Christ; there was an abandonment about it, and such an utter forgetfulness of the whole world but him, and merging of all he wished or hoped for into the affection of that single bosom, that we never in imagination can behold his head resting upon it in childlike happiness, as if life had nothing more to give, without the deepest emotion.

There is a certain sadness connected with the attachment of two friends who have become so much to each other, that they divide the world in only two parts, "one where the loved object is, and one where it is not." It is too intense for this life; changes and separation will weaken it, or death disrupt it. But there is something sadder in the attachment of Christ and John. The deep devotion, the pure and generous heart, the tender sympathy, the trusting, loving nature of the latter, had so won upon the Saviour, that every look he cast upon him was a caress, and every word he spoke, took the gentle tone of a mother addressing her child. He knew how his disciple loved him, and knew too how much he must suffer in the sufferings that awaited him. John, absorbed by his attachment, his countenance by turns made tearful and joyous at the kind words and glorious truths that fell from his Master's lips, seemed never to dream of approaching evil, of possible separation. Jesus, on the other hand, as he with his sorrowful face looked down upon him leaning contentedly on his breast, thought of the future. With his human heart beating warmly for the true devoted friend on his bosom, he could not but sigh, knowing, as he did, the trials and sufferings his tender nature must yet pass through to prove its love for him. As, in imagination, I behold the two in each other's embrace, I seem to see tears on the cheeks of Jesus, at the same time that his hand bestows a caress. The implicit confidence and trust of his follower appealed to every noble quality of the heart, and he must in those moments have looked upon John, as a mother upon the smiles of her infant, when she knows that in a few hours the executioner's axe will leave it an orphan in the world. The dark hints he ever and anon threw out, filled John with wonder, rather than anxiety, and he loved on, indifferent to his own fate. The other disciples respected this attachment, and, far from being jealous, seemed affected by it. When Christ uttered those sad words, "One of you shall betray me," they dared not ask him who it was, but requested John, who they knew would not be rebuked, to do it for them. *He*, looking up from that pillow he *could* not surrender to any other head, said, "Lord, who is it?" and the Saviour told him. The youngest of all, a mere youth when he began to follow Christ, he was yet most beloved of all.

John must have passed through strange states of mind, as the wondrous character of the being he loved so intimately and treated so familiarly, became revealed to him in his miracles and by his high claims. Christ seems always to choose him for a companion when about to accomplish any great event. John heard his predictions respecting Jerusalem and the Jewish nation; stood by when he took the hand of the dead daughter of Jairus, and bade her arise amid her astonished friends; was one of the three who ascended the Mount of Transfiguration, and saw the face and form he had so often caressed assume the likeness and splendor of God; was in the garden on that night of fearful agony, and gazed on that pallid face streaked with blood which had so often and so kindly smiled on him; and, last of all, beheld him ascend into Heaven, triumphant over death and the grave.

But there is one event which gives John peculiar claims to being "that disciple whom Jesus loved." Christ had endured the agony in the garden; his sacred face had been spit upon; his cheek shamefully struck; the farce and insult of a trial endured; he had fainted under the cross as he struggled with it up the steep hill-side; and, with his frame strung to the point of extremest sensibility, had been laid on the rough beams, and the bolts rudely crushed through his shrinking hands and feet, and thus suspended on high. Around him was the railing crowd, beside him a scoffing thief. All his friends had forsaken him and fled; and alone, all alone, he was left to wrestle with his doom. No, not quite alone, for nearer the cross than the taunting rabble stood his mother. It was *her child*, bleeding and dying there before her eyes, and what were the scoffs and violence of those around her! ay, what was death itself compared to the throes of maternal anguish that shook her bosom! There stood John, rivaling even the mother in love. He forgot he had a life to lose; he did not even hear the taunts that were rained upon him, nor see the fingers of scorn that were pointed at his tears; he saw only his dying friend and Lord; beheld but the bosom on which he had so often rested his head, heaving and swelling as though the heart would burst its confinement, and the brow on which peace ever sat like a white-winged dove, contracted with agony unutterable. True to the last, pale as the suffering being before him, he stood and wept in speechless sorrow. Christ, in the midst of his torture, and in the midst of his stupendous scheme he was finishing at such a fearful price, cut off from earth, and just as Heaven too was about to abandon him, and the power of his Father was darkening over his spirit, was struck with this matchless love. The last, the wildest wave that ever broke over the soul of the Saviour, was gathering for its flow, yet even then he gazed lovingly on those two faithful hearts, and his calm though failing voice reached their ears, and he said to his mother, "Behold thy son," and to John, "Behold thy mother." True-hearted disciple, faithful friend, take *my* place beside my mother; to *thy love*, so great for me, I can safely commit her. Oh! what a proof of confidence and attachment was that! So high an honor was never before paid human love. Oh! what an inheritance was that the Son of God gave him,—his mother, and his affectionate confidence in the last hour of his suffering, and while standing on the portals of the eternal kingdom. No wonder that John, after that, took her to his own home, soothed her sorrows, nursed her declining years, and at last gently and sorrowfully laid her in her grave.

Years passed by, and changes and persecution came, but no change in the affection of John for his Master. Living in *his life*, he now lived to make known his death and resurrection. Love seemed to supply the place of native energy, and he passed into Asia, preaching the gospel, and planting churches, until at length the hand of persecution reached him also, and he was banished to a lonely island in the Ægean Sea.

How long he remained there we know not; silence and uncertainty rest on his history. Alone he trod the desolate beach, cheered by no voice, solaced by no companionship. He whose happiness had consisted in laying his head on the bosom of his friend and Lord, was left without a friend. The monotonous dash of waves at his feet, the broad and boundless deep stretching away before him, the cry of the sea bird and the roar of the storm, these were the only sights and sounds left to the lonely exile. Day after day, and week after week, the same unvarying routine. The solitary walk on the shore, and still more solitary rest under an overhanging rock, filled up the measure of his employments. Ah, how sweet then was the remembrance of his long and affectionate interviews with Christ—how full of solace the words he had spoken, so sweet that the desert seemed peopled with angels, and the hoarse murmur of the sea sounded like an anthem of praise to God. As he stood and saw the sun go down on the deep, he remembered that just so it flashed over the Sea of Tiberias, when Jesus fed the five thousand. As he looked up to the silent firmament, gorgeous with stars, he remembered the strange night he passed with Jesus on Mount Tabor, looking on the same heavens; and when he pillowed his lonely head upon the sand, he thought, with throbbing heart, of him "who had not where to lay his head.

How long he lived thus in holy contemplation, to prepare him for the wondrous revelations about to be made, we know not; but, one Sabbath morning, as he was walking the desert island, filled with thoughts of the world to come, he heard a voice repeating in trumpet tones behind him, "I am Alpha and Omega, the first and the last." Turning to meet the voice, he saw a form dread enough to appal the stoutest heart. A mantle wrapped it from the neck to the feet; the head and hair were white as wool, the eyes burned like fire, the feet shone like brass in a furnace; in his uplifted hand seven stars were blazing; his countenance was like the *sun shining in its strength*, and his voice like "the *sound of many waters*." No wonder the overwhelmed exile fell on his face as a dead man, before this fearful form and aspect, and dared not lift his eyes again from the earth, till the same terrible voice bade him arise. Of the wondrous visions that were then revealed to him, who can speak? The gates of hell and heaven were flung open to his view. He saw the smoke that curtained the bottomless pit, and the city whose only light is the presence of the Lamb; but the speechless agony, the terrific conflicts, the appalling sights, together with the splendors of the heaven of heavens, the throne and the white-vested elders, the dazzling glory of the crystal sea and rivers of paradise, the music of the harpers, the thrilling power of that loud hallelujah, "Worthy is the Lamb that was slain," as it rolled from ten times ten thousand tongues full on the throne of God and the Lamb, who can describe? That desolate island around John, was greater than Mount Carmel of old, when horses and chariots of fire encircled the prophet. God was there! unveiling himself, this world, and eternity, to a mortal.

This strange interview, with its long train of mysterious and fearful visions, was at last ended; as was also the exile of John, and he smiled once more in the midst of his friends. But the scenes he had passed through did not change his nature; he was the same gentle, loving being as ever. Overflowing with kindness and sympathy, all things else seemed worthless in comparison.

And when the lamp of light burned dimly, and his trembling voice could hardly articulate, he still spoke of *love.* It is said he lived to be eighty years of age, and then, too feeble to walk, was carried into church on men's shoulders, and, though scarcely able to speak, would faintly murmur, "Brethren, love one another." Affection was his life, and it seemed to him that the world could be governed by *love.*

CHAPTER XI.

PAUL.

The history of our race furnishes some few men who are like those mountain summits which repose in light, while all below is in deep shadow. To me, Moses, *independent* of the inspiration he received from Heaven, is the grandest man the race has produced. Intellectually, he towers above all before and after him. The level ray which should leave his forehead would gild but few brows on the earth. By it we might see the faces of Elijah, David, and Isaiah, but scarce another till we came to Paul.

Paul, in his natural character before his conversion, resembles Bonaparte more than any other man—I mean both in his intellectual developments and energy of will. He had the same inflexibility of purpose, the same utter indifference to human sufferings when he had once determined on his course, the same tireless, unconquerable resolution, the same fearlessness both of man's power and opinions, and that calm self-reliance and mysterious control over others. But the point of greatest resemblance is in the union of a strong, correct judgment, with rapidity of thought and sudden impulse. They thought quicker, yet better than other men. The power, too, which both possessed was all *practical* power. There are many men of strong minds, whose force nevertheless wastes itself in reflection, or in theories for others to act upon. Thought may work out into language, but not into action. They will *plan* better than they can perform. But these two men not only *thought* better, but they could work better than all other men. I have made this comparison because this great *practical* power is of rare occurrence. An astonishing head and an astonishing arm are seldom united.

The birthplace of Paul was well adapted to the formation of such a character as his. Born on the Mediterranean, with its broad and ever-heaving bosom before him, and an impenetrable barrier of mountains behind him, his mind early took its stern character and lofty bearing, and in his youth he exhibited those qualities which afterwards made him such a fearful and wonderful man. He had scarcely completed his studies, before he plunged into the most exciting scenes of those times. The new religion, professing to have the long-promised Messiah for its founder, agitated the entire nation. To the proud young scholar, those ignorant fishermen, disputing with the doctors of law, and claiming for their religion a superiority over his, which had been transmitted through a hundred generations, and been sanctioned by a thousand miracles and wonders, were objects of the deepest scorn. Filled with indignation, and panting for action, he threw himself boldly into the struggle, and became foremost in the persecution that followed.

With a stern brow and an unflinching eye, he stood by and saw Stephen stoned to death. Arrested by no obstacles, softened by no suffering, he roamed the streets of Jerusalem like a fiend, breaking even into the retirement of the Christian's home, dragging thence women and children, and casting them into prison. Though young in years, he had the nerve of a hoary-headed tyrant, and before his relentless will every thing went down.

I have often wondered how his hatred and rage could hold out in his long journey to Damascus. The silence and solitude of nature, her quiet aspect and lovely scenes, as he passed along, should have subdued, or at least allayed his hostility. Especially at night, when he pitched his tent on some green hill-side, and saw the sun go down in a sea of green, and felt the balmy breeze of evening, redolent with the perfume of flowers, softly kissing his brow; and later, perchance, listened to the note of the bulbul filling the moonlight with melody, it must have required nerves of iron to resist the soothing influences around him. Yet, young as he was, and hence peculiarly open to all the beauties of nature, he never seems a moment to have vacillated in his purpose.

The same self-control and perfect subjection of his emotions—even terror itself—to the mandates of his will, are exhibited in his conduct when smitten to the earth, and blinded by the light and voice from Heaven. John, when arrested by the same voice on the Isle of Patmos, fell on his face as a dead man, and dared not stir or speak till encouraged by the language, "Fear not." But Paul (or Saul), though a persecutor, and violent man, showed no symptoms of alarm or terror. The voice, the blow, the light, the glory, and the darkness that followed, were sufficient to upset the strongest mind; but he, master of himself and his emotions, instead of giving way to exclamations of terror, simply said: "Lord, what wilt thou have me to do?" With his reason and judgment as steady and strong as ever, he knew at once that something was wanted of him, and, ever ready to act, he asked what it was.

From this moment we cease to contemplate him in his natural character alone. When the persecutor becomes the persecuted, and the proud young scholar the humble, despised disciple of Jesus of Nazareth, and leaving the halls of the wise and proud, and companionship of dignitaries, casts his lot in with ignorant fishermen, he becomes a different being. His mental characteristics, his resolute will, fearless heart, and tireless energy, are the same; but his moral nature, how changed!

From this time on, his track can be distinguished by the commotions about it, and the light above it. Straight back to Jerusalem, from whence he had so recently come with letters to legalize his persecutions, he went, to cast his lot in with those he had followed with violence and slaughter. His strong heart never beat one quicker pulsation through fear, when the lofty turrets of the proud city flashed on his vision. Neither did he steal away to the dark alleys and streets, where the disciples were concealed, and tell them secretly his faith in the Son of God. He strode into the synagogues, and before the astonished priests preached Christ and him crucified. He thundered at the door of the Sanhedrim itself, and shaking Jerusalem like an earthquake, awoke a tempest of rage and fury on himself. With assassins dogging his footsteps, he at length left the city. But, instead of going to places where he was unknown, and where his feelings would be less tried, he started for his native city, his father's house, the home of his boyhood, for his kindred and friends. To entreaties, tears, scorn, and violence, he was alike impervious. To Antioch and Cyprus, along the coast of Syria to Greece and Rome, over the known world he went like a blazing comet, waking up the nations of the earth. From the top of Mars' Hill, with the gorgeous city at his feet, and the Acropolis and Parthenon behind him; on the deck of his shattered vessel in the intervals of the crash of billows, in the gloomy walls of a prison, on the borders of the eternal kingdom, he speaks in the same calm and determined tone. Deterred by no danger, awed by no presence, and shrinking from no responsibility, he moves before us like some grand embodiment of power. The nations heave around him, and kings turn pale in his presence. Bands of conspirators swear neither to eat nor drink till they have slain him, rulers and priests combine against him, the people stone him; yet, over the din of the conflict and storm of violence, his voice of eloquence rises clear and distinct as a trumpet-call, as he still preaches Christ and him crucified. The whip is laid on his back till the blood starts with every blow, and then his mangled body is thrown into a dungeon; but at midnight you hear that same calm strong voice which has shaken the world, poured forth in a hymn of praise to God, and lo! an earthquake rocks the prison to its foundations; the manacles fall from the hands of the captives, the bolts withdraw of themselves, and the massive doors swing back on their hinges. Finding that the whip, the dungeon, the assassin's knife, and the executioner's sword cannot move him from his purpose, the world point in scorn to the cross, to signify that the Christ he preaches died the death of a felon. "The cross, the cross," they sneeringly exclaim, to bring the blush of shame to his cheek; but, to their astonishment, they hear him shout louder than they all, "The cross, the cross, I glory in the cross." On the very spot they have selected for his confusion, he plants himself, and, with one arm around the emblem of disgrace, and the other pointed to Heaven, he makes the hill of Crucifixion burn like the gates of Paradise. Nay more, he goes and stands by that felon's tomb—Him they call a felon — and preaches the resurrection of the dead.

I can never in imagination behold him, with his somewhat diminutive form, his head slightly bald, nose aquiline, and eyes dark and flashing, in the presence of Felix, sweeping every thing down in his torrent-like eloquence, without feeling my heart beat with a quicker motion. In a gorgeous apartment, filled with the noble and the gay, who have assembled from curiosity, he stands to defend himself against the charges of the orator Tertullus. He listens to the opprobrious epithets of "pestilent fellow," "ringleader of a sect of Nazarenes," "profaner of the temple," with a composed countenance, until bid to answer for himself. At first calm, dignified, and respectful, he repels the accusations; then, taking fire as he touches upon the loftier topic of the resurrection of the dead, he forgets all but the cause he advocates. But, especially, when Felix would hear farther, and he "reasoned of righteousness, temperance, and a judgment to come," does he rise before us like a being from another world. After explaining the law, its justice and purity, till the reason of his listeners was convinced, he spoke of its claims in man and on them—showed how sinful and corrupt their lives had been, then passed to the judgment of the great day, and its just and fearful retributions.

As his imagination kindled on this stupendous theme, forgot was all—the noble audience before him, his bonds, imprisonment, and coming fate. Those massive walls sink away before the descending God; the Archangel's trumpet is heard pealing the knell of time; the dead come forth; the throne is set, and before it all the nations of the earth are gathered, awaiting their doom. Gone is the look of indifference and smile of incredulity; gone even the sneer of Tertullus; and a solemn silence, broken only by the tones of the fearful speaker, reigns through the vast apartment. No wonder, when he closed, the haughty Felix trembled.

But stern as Paul was amid his foes, and lofty in his course, he nevertheless had a heart full of the tenderest emotions. A *truer* never beat in a human bosom. At times his natural fierceness would break forth, as when the high priest ordered him to be smitten contrary to the law. Turning like a lion upon him, he thundered in his astonished ears, "God shall smite thee, thou whited wall." Yet he was ready in a moment to be just; and there never was before so fearless and inflexible a nature joined with so much tenderness of heart. Look at his parting with his friends at Ephesus, when on his way to Jerusalem! How touching his address, and how characteristic! In closing, he said, "And now

I go bound in the spirit to Jerusalem, not knowing the things that shall befall me there, save that in every city bonds and imprisonment await me." "In every city" the same hard fate; "yet none of these things," he says, "move me, neither count I my life dear unto me, so that I might finish my course with joy, and the ministry which I have received of the Lord Jesus, to testify the gospel of the grace of God." None of these things moved him — no, these were trifling matters, bonds, imprisonment, and death; *duty*, the salvation of man, the honor of God, these alone filled him with anxiety, and nerved him to action. Of one thing, however, he told them he was convinced, and that was, that they "should see his face no more." To them he appealed as witnesses, that he had labored faithfully for their welfare, and then, kneeling down on the shore, prayed with them. How often have I wished that that prayer had come down to us. One thing, however, I know, it was full of self-forgetfulness and fervent pleading for those who knelt around him. No wonder, when it was finished, they fell on his neck and kissed him, "sorrowing most of all for the words, *they should see his face no more.*" It would be a long, long time before they could find another so brave and affectionate a heart—one that would dare all things, and suffer all things for them. They doubtless besought him to stay with them, and be comforted by their sympathy and love. But no, though bonds and imprisonment awaited him in *every city*, none of these things moved him. On to his fate, not sadly, reluctantly, but serenely, *joyfully* he went, thinking only of fulfilling the ministry he had received. Calm, dignified, and resolved, he took the path of duty with an unfaltering step. No malice or threats of his foes could deter him from laboring for their welfare; no insults prevent his prayer in their behalf; no wrongs heaped on his innocent head keep back his forgiveness.

One cannot point to a single spot in his whole career, where he faltered a moment, or gave way to discouragement or fear. Through all his perilous life, he exhibited the same intrepidity of character and lofty spirit. With his eye fixed on regions beyond the ken of ordinary mortals, and kindling on glories it was not permitted him to reveal, he pressed forward to an incorruptible crown, a fadeless kingdom. And then his death, how indescribably sublime. Napoleon, dying in the midst of the midnight storm, with the last words that fell from his lips a battle cry, and his passing spirit watching in its delirium the torn heads of his mighty columns, as they disappeared in the smoke of the conflict, is a sight that awes and startles us. But behold Paul also, a war-worn veteran, battered with many a scar, though in a spiritual warfare, looking back, not with alarm, but transport; gazing not on the earth, but on Heaven. Hear his calm, serene voice ringing over the storms and commotions of life: "I am now ready to be offered, and the time of my departure is at hand. I have fought a good fight, I have finished my course, there is laid up for me a crown of righteousness. No shouts of foemen, nor smoke or carnage of battle surrounded his spirit struggling to be free; but troops of shining angels, the smile of God, and the songs of the redeemed, these guarded him and welcomed him home.

CHAPTER XII.

THE TOMB OF CHRIST.

WHILE Jesus of Nazareth lived, nothing seemed able to subdue the malice of his foes. The less cause he gave for their hatred, the greater it became. If he had been guilty of the charges brought against him, they would of course have put him to death, while the vindication of his innocence only strengthened and quickened their bloody purpose. He sought no man's gold or silver, he inflicted no evil—but poor and self-denying, devoted all his time and efforts to the benefit of others; yet his conduct did not soften the hearts of his enemies. When the band of soldiers came upon him on Mount Olivet, the ghastly and blood-streaked face, and utter exhaustion and lonely condition of the sufferer, awoke no commiseration. Though he stood in the Judgment Hall of Pilate like a "lamb before his shearers," his gentle aspect could not prevent the rude buffet, or his sacred face from being spit upon. His meek obedience could not save his back from the whip, nor his kind, forgiving look keep the thorns from his temples. His hard fate could not find a sympathetic chord in the bosom of those who sought his life, and when he fainted under the cross, they were only fearful lest the overtasked frame should give out before they had inflicted on it greater torture. His unutterable agony—even the "Father, forgive them!" which has since thrilled the heart of the world, awoke no remorse in their hearts. They clamored more fiercely for *his* life, who was praying for them and theirs, than for the thieves by his side. Through the hands, opened only to bless, they smote the nails, and on the agony, borne solely for their redemption, they railed in mockery. And even after death they drove the spear into his side, though the silent language he uttered to them was, "There is an easier and better way to my heart than by the spear."

All this did not move them; but at last malice and hate had done their worst. They had been allowed to insult, to torture, and at last to slay, and there was nothing more for them to do. The victim was beyond their reach, and so, with ribald songs and shouts, they moved away, and left the dead Christ hanging on the cross. But a wealthy counsellor, who had secretly loved Jesus, went to Pilate and begged the body. Sadly and silently he took it down, and laid it in a new tomb. He and Nicodemus bending over the lifeless form, paying the last sad tokens of respect to him they loved, composing the limbs decently for the grave, is a sight that not only soothes but startles us. *For the grave* they are preparing him. Do they really think then that he is dead for ever, that nothing but the archangel's trump will waken him again?

He is dead, and the stillness of night has settled on his lonely sepulchre in the garden. A rock closes the entrance, and the great drama is over. Sad, sad is the fate of the little band of Christians. They have forsaken friends and home, endured privations, abuse, and torture; and now stand the objects of universal scorn, for their attachment to one who has left them nothing but his grave. Wanderers on the wide earth, they are like "sheep without a shepherd." The form they worshiped is wrapped in the shroud, the lips on which they hung in tears of rapture are sealed in death. The hope of the world is vanished, the light that was rising on its darkness, quenched for ever; for there, in that tomb, cold and dead, rests the body of him who called himself the "Son of God." The arm that claimed to uphold the universe, has been stretched upon the cross, and now lies stark and stiff beside its owner, and the tongue that declared it could with a word bring "legions of angels" from on high, is now dumb and powerless. Leaning over the dead Lazarus, he, with a simple command, had raised him from corruption. The sheeted dead obeyed his call, and the charnel-house stirred with living men at his voice; but no motion or life is within *his* sepulchre; darkness covers it. "He saved others, himself he cannot save." Perchance the angels were in the same state of uncertainty as men, and the melancholy echo came back from the skies, "Christ is dead! *we are orphans! all orphans!*" The star that shone over the manger of Bethlehem was a mockery.

The sun shrouding itself in darkness and the earthquake rending the globe, both attested how dire, how irremediable was the calamity.

The long-expected Messiah, the King of Israel is no more. A whole day has he lain in the tomb; soon dust will begin to crumble back to dust; and now darkness has again fallen on the world. The stars are gently twinkling in the sky, the evening wind sweeps carelessly by, the hum of the distant town is gradually dying away, and all nature moves on as peacefully as though Christ were not dead. The branches are swaying, and the flowers are nodding around that quiet grave, and one cannot dream of the scene that will transpire there before the morning dawns. Nothing uncommon marks the hour or the place, save that two Roman sentinels stand silent in the moonlight, which flashes on their steel helmets and polished spears. The clank of their armor is heard at intervals in the stillness; all else rests undisturbed as the sleeping world around. 'Tis past midnight, and the morn is already hanging over the western hills, when suddenly darkness wraps the shuddering earth. The ground begins to heave beneath that sepulchre, and lo, an earthquake thunders on. Rocks are rent, graves open, and the reanimated dead come forth and gaze once more on the heavens. In the midst of this elemental war, and commotion, and gloom, a form, clad in vesture white as snow, and with a countenance that outflashes the lightning, is seen cleaving the darkness. The throbbing earth and troubled heavens are forgotten before his burning presence, and the sentinels fall as dead men at the door of the sepulchre they are guarding. He rolls back the stone, and Jesus of Nazareth stands erect before him. He has conquered death and the grave, and leaving behind the garments that wrapped him, steps forth into the night. But the place in which he has lain is still held sacred; for two angels, clad in white, sit, one at the head, the other at the foot of the tomb, watching. The earth has slept, but Heaven been wakeful, on this fearful night.

The armed soldiers fallen on their faces —an angel sitting on the stone rolled back from the door—two celestial beings leaning over the tomb within—these were the objects that met the gaze at early dawn. What a scene for that quiet garden! On that night, and on that little spot, were secured the resurrection of the body and the redemption of the soul. No wonder angels leaned thoughtfully there.

How strange must the spectacle have appeared to Mary Magdalene. The penitent's heart still yearned towards her forgiving Lord. She had stood near the cross and seen him die; she had discovered the place of his burial and lingered long and anxiously about it. Before the day dawned she had risen from her sleepless couch, and stolen out in the darkness to weep there. Scornful eyes could no longer watch her; no voice reproach her; even the Roman soldiers would respect so great a sorrow, and not deny her the poor boon of weeping on the spot where her Lord was entombed. With a heart bursting with grief, and perhaps a strange, undefined hope in her breast, she threaded her way through the garden to the sepulchre. Perhaps the rumbling of the earthquake, so like that which closed the crucifixion scene, had roused her before day, and she expected some new manifestation from Heaven. If so, she was not disappointed. The open sepulchre, with a strange, bright being near the door—two angels within, sitting by the empty tomb—the risen Saviour standing before her—the lifeless sentinels in the midst, might well confuse her senses so that she did not recognise the Saviour until he spoke.

The wonderful news soon spread on every side; and Peter, ever impulsive and headlong, came, with the speed of wind, to ascertain the truth. The sepulchre was open, the tomb was there, and the grave-clothes folded upon it, but the inmate was gone and the angels had departed. It was a deserted sepulchre, and the solitude and mystery that wrapped it must have fallen with strange power on the heart of Peter.

How rapidly events had followed each other. The betrayal, trial, and crucifixion, preceded but a few hours the burial; in a few hours more the dead awoke and moved about among his friends. A few days passed away, and the dead, buried, and risen Saviour ascended the heavens. Now the Christian may go back to that grave, around which he wept unavailing tears, and smile in rapture. Its darkness has turned into day, and its solemn depths are filled with angelic voices singing the "resurrection and the life."

Centuries rolled by, and that tomb became a ruin amid ruins. The infidel sneered at the poor pilgrim as he knelt beside it in tears, and chased him away with the lash. Years passed, and Europe awoke as from a dream at the insult heaped upon the sepulchre of the Saviour. At the preaching of Peter the Hermit, Christendom was moved as it never before had been. A crusade was set on foot to redeem that sepulchre, and in a year six millions of souls had volunteered for the Holy War. Old men, women, and children, the rich and poor, were seen streaming by tens of thousands towards the sacred spot. Kings and princes, and warriors of renown, buried their feuds, forgot their career of worldly glory, and, striking hands together, swore that the sword should never return to the scabbard till the tomb of Christ was delivered from the hands of the infidel. One desire animated every heart, one purpose filled every bosom; the contagion spread from house to house and kingdom to kingdom. "It became an enthusiasm, a passion, a madness." Nearly a quarter of a million fell on the very threshold of the undertaking. Yet an army of six hundred thousand men at length stood in gorgeous array on the plains of Asia, and, with waving banners and pealing trumpets, began to hew their way to the tomb of Christ. Swept away by famine, pestilence, and the sword, they still pressed on till but half of their number was left to fling themselves on the walls of Jerusalem. Behold them at length approaching Bethlehem. A deputation of Christians go forth to meet them, and in a moment that weary, wasted army is moved like the forest by a sudden wind. *Bethlehem* is before them, the place where the Saviour was born. The name awoke a thousand touching associations, and thrilled every heart with strange rapture. That night the excited host could not sleep; and at midnight took up their line of march for Jerusalem. In dead silence—many with bare feet and uncovered heads—pressed tremblingly on through the darkness. At length, the sun, with that suddenness which always accompanies an eastern dawn, rushed into the heavens, and there lay Jerusalem before them. The object of all their toils, for which they had endured famine and pestilence, and been mowed down by the sword of the infidel, the one bright object of their lives, smiling in summer beauty at their feet. There was Mount Olivet, there Mount Calvary, and there, too, the sepulchre of the Saviour. Oh! who can describe the emotions that then swept through that Christian host? Some knelt down and prayed, others leaped, shouting, into the air; the mailed knight sobbed like an infant; until at length the murmur, Jerusalem! arose at first faint and low, like the far off sound of the sea, but gradually swelling to the full voiced thunder, till "Jerusalem! Jerusalem!" filled all the air, and rolled gloriously to the heavens. Then, taking fire at the thought that the holy city and sacred tomb were in the hands of unbelievers, they raised their battle-cry and went pouring forward on the walls, like the inrolling tide of the sea.

What a spectacle the crusade presented! The old and the young, the sage and the ignorant, the king and the serf, the knight and the recluse, women and children, the pure and the impure, all pressing forward to one goal—the tomb of Christ. The plains of Asia covered with magnificent armies, and on every banner that waved over them, the *cross of Christ.* Ten thousand knights spurring joyfully to the onset, every lance set in rest for the *honor of Christ.* Across trackless deserts, over rugged mountains and bloody battle-fields, through disease and death, still onward to the *tomb of Christ.* Angels watched that tomb after the Saviour had left it. Mary worshiped there; the pilgrim for centuries scourged himself before it; the chivalry of the world battled around it, and the heart of the world still throbs at the mention of its name.

To the Christian it will ever be an object of the deepest interest; not merely because it was consecrated by the form of the Son of God, but because, as he looks on its emptiness, he feels assured of the resurrection of the dead. He who laid there "is the *first-fruits of them that sleep.*"

THE END.

www.ingramcontent.com/pod-product-compliance
Lightning Source LLC
LaVergne TN
LVHW011208110826
845150LV00006B/1358